Have we arrived at a New World Disorder? Well, the UK is no longer a stabilizing power in Europe, and the US has stopped functioning as a stabilizer in the global system. Behind these structural changes we find the manifold failures of neoliberal economics. In the footsteps of Keynes, Polanyi and Habermas, Heikki Patomäki uncovers the causes and dynamics of these complex crises, and also identifies the keys of a progressive project that can save the legacy of enlightenment and democratic politics in Europe, as well as the world system, and help to find the way back to social progress.

– **László Andor**, *Former EU Commissioner for Employment, Social Affairs and Inclusion*

Disintegrative Tendencies in Global Political Economy

Whether we talk about human learning and unlearning, securitization, or political economy, the forces and mechanisms generating both globalization and disintegration are causally efficacious across the world. Thus, the processes that led to the victory of the 'Leave' campaign in the June 2016 referendum on UK European Union membership are not simply confined to the United Kingdom, or even Europe. Similarly, conflict in Ukraine and the presidency of Donald Trump hold implications for a stage much wider than EU–Russia or the United States alone.

Patomäki explores the world-historical mechanisms and processes that have created the conditions for the world's current predicaments and, arguably, involve potential for better futures. Operationally, he relies on the philosophy of dialectical critical realism and on the methods of contemporary social sciences, exploring how crises, learning and politics are interwoven through uneven wealth-accumulation and problematical growth-dynamics. Seeking to illuminate the causes of the currently prevailing tendencies towards disintegration, antagonism and – ultimately – war, he also shows how these developments are in fact embedded in deeper processes of human learning. The book embraces a Wellsian warning about the increasingly likely possibility of a military disaster, but its central objective is to further enlightenment and holoreflexivity within the current world-historical conjuncture.

This work will be of interest to students and scholars of international relations, peace research, security studies and international political economy.

Heikki Patomäki is Professor of World Politics at the University of Helsinki, Finland.

Rethinking Globalizations
Edited by Barry K. Gills,
University of Helsinki, Finland
Kevin Gray,
University of Sussex, UK.

This series is designed to break new ground in the literature on globalization and its academic and popular understanding. Rather than perpetuating or simply reacting to the economic understanding of globalization, this series seeks to capture the term and broaden its meaning to encompass a wide range of issues and disciplines and convey a sense of alternative possibilities for the future.

For more information, please visit: https://www.routledge.com/Rethinking-Globalizations/book-series/RG

Environmental Security in Transnational Contexts
What Relevance for Regional Human Security Regimes?
Edited by Harlan Koff and Carmen Maganda

Disintegrative Tendencies in Global Political Economy
Exits and Conflicts
Heikki Patomäki

Brexit and the Political Economy of Fragmentation
Things Fall Apart
Edited by Jamie Morgan & Heikki Patomäki

Chinese Labour in the Global Economy
Capitalist Exploitation and Strategies of Resistance
Edited by Andreas Bieler and Chun-Yi Lee

From International Relations to World Civilizations
The contributions of Robert W. Cox
Edited by Shannon Brincat

Disintegrative Tendencies in Global Political Economy
Exits and Conflicts

Heikki Patomäki

First published 2018
by Routledge
2 Park Square, Milton Park, Abingdon, Oxon OX14 4RN

and by Routledge
711 Third Avenue, New York, NY 10017

Routledge is an imprint of the Taylor & Francis Group, an informa business

© 2018 Heikki Patomäki

The right of Heikki Patomäki to be identified as author of this work has been asserted by him in accordance with sections 77 and 78 of the Copyright, Designs and Patents Act 1988.

The Open Access version of this book, available at www.taylorfrancis.com, has been made available under a Creative Commons Attribution-Non Commercial-No Derivatives 4.0 license.

Trademark notice: Product or corporate names may be trademarks or registered trademarks, and are used only for identification and explanation without intent to infringe.

British Library Cataloguing-in-Publication Data
A catalogue record for this book is available from the British Library

Library of Congress Cataloging-in-Publication Data
A catalog record for this book has been requested

ISBN: 978-1-138-06530-7 (hbk)
ISBN: 978-0-367-35757-3 (pbk)
ISBN: 978-1-315-15979-9 (ebk)

Typeset in Times New Roman by
Apex CoVantage, LLC

Contents

List of figures		viii
List of tables		ix
Acknowledgements		x
1	Introduction: the world falling apart	1
2	Brexit and the causes of European disintegration	16
3	EU, Russia and the conflict in Ukraine	41
4	Trumponomics and the logic of global disintegration	70
5	Piketty's inequality $r > g$: the key to understanding and overcoming the dynamics of disintegration	94
6	Conclusion: holoreflexivity and the shape of things to come	113
	Index	135

Figures

1.1	The self-reinforcing negative dynamics of the neoliberal world economy	5
2.1	Politico-economic developments, social-psychological mechanisms and cognitive schemes	23
2.2	The rising popularity of UKIP	27
3.1	Ukraine's GDP per capita and growth rate	53
3.2	Ukraine's current account balance and foreign reserves	54
3.3	A two-phase causal mechanism leading to securitization and other-blaming	56
4.1	Income inequality: top 1 percent and bottom 90 percent average pre-tax incomes, 1949–2014	74
4.2	Wealth inequality: top 1 percent and bottom 90 percent average wealth, 1949–2014	74
4.3	Manufacturing, value added (% of GDP)	75
4.4	Manufacturing employees and real output	76
5.1	World GDP per capita growth rates	98
5.2	High-income countries' GDP per capita growth rates	98

Tables

2.1	Four ethico-political alternatives in European politics	20
2.2	The Eurozone output growth and unemployment rate	31
4.1	Six scenarios about the effects of Trumponomics, especially in trade	84

Acknowledgements

In June 2016, Barry Gills asked Jamie Morgan and me to guest-edit a special forum on Brexit for *Globalizations*, and it was in that context that the idea for this monograph emerged, only a few weeks after the British referendum.

Both Barry and Jamie have played important roles in the process that brought this manuscript into being. Chapter 2 has benefitted from the work on Brexit forums. A couple of paragraphs at the beginning of that chapter have been adopted from our "Introduction: Special Forum on Brexit", *Globalizations* (14):1, 2017, pp. 99–103. The two Brexit forums will be eventually compiled into a book and published in December 2017 as a single edited volume in Routledge's Globalizations series. Moreover, Jamie not only read Chapter 2, providing most useful comments, but after the finalization of the manuscript he also helped me to shorten the text by thousands of words to meet the requirements of the Focus-series.

Parts of Chapters 4 and 5 have been published in two special issues of *Real-World Economics Review* (the one on Piketty in issue 69 and the one on "Trumponomics" in 79), edited by Edward Fullbrook and Jamie; both of these two issues have been republished as books. The newer version of the second half of Chapter 4 was originally written with Barry, but appears here in a shortened, modified, updated and recontextualized form. James Galbraith's critical remarks helped me to clarify some of the main points of Chapter 5.

Chapter 3 has a different history, although it ties into the analysis of the other chapters very closely. I presented the first version of it on 16 September 2016 as "EU's role in the Evolvement of the Russia–West Conflict and Outbreak of War in Ukraine", at the EuroMemorandum conference in Coimbra, Portugal. I am thankful to the participants of the panel "EU-external relations: Destabilizing the Neighbours" for comments. Most importantly, however, I have benefitted from the comments of my old friend Tuomas Forsberg, who forced me to explicate the argument much better, and Dmytro

Khutkyy, who happened to be visiting Helsinki at the time that I was finalizing the chapter and helped me in making the argument more nuanced.

It would not have been possible to put together all these elements into a tight and coherent book form so quickly and proficiently without the competent assistance of Markus Ristola. With the generosity of the Faculty of Social Sciences, Markus served as my full-time research assistant from April to June 2017. Thank you, Markus! In addition, all the chapters have been language- and copy-edited in a very professional and efficient manner by Kenneth Quek.

As always, it goes without saying that I am responsible for all the remaining errors and for what may turn out as non-adequate truth-judgements (as we critical realists know, the preface paradox is no paradox at all, as an author may be quite sure that her book will be revealed to contain errors but be quite unable to say what they are just now).

In Helsinki, 31 July 2017
Heikki Patomäki

1 Introduction
The world falling apart

This book is a warning about the likely consequences of disintegrative tendencies in the global political economy. It is vital to formulate this warning in a self-critical manner. Often, the perception "I have been watching the news and the world seems to be falling apart" is illusory. Media images of wars, threats of violence and senseless terror, and the consequent precautionary actions of security apparatuses, conceal that the world is on average less violent now than past centuries or millennia.[1]

Sensationalized news about wars in the Middle East and the Ukrainian conflict in Europe, and political developments such as Brexit and the election of Donald Trump, have intensified the sense that things are falling apart. Many commentators convey a common fear of impending global disorder. Alarm is often connected to historical stories about the decline of the West and the rise of a post-Western world.

Extrapolation from news can be a misleading way to understand the world. As Steven Pinker explains, news is "always about events that happened and not about things that didn't happen" (Belluz 2016). News media focus selectively on the dramatic and tend to push non-dramatic events and slow processes to the background. Headlines do not usually scream that violent death has become rare. In Western Europe and North America, as well, the absolute number of people killed in terrorist attacks has been in decline for decades, despite notable events – Paris, November 2015 or 9/11.[2]

Furthermore, theories may be more historical and processual than everyday commercial news but can be equally misleading. For example, the typical alarmist reaction to President Trump resonates with hegemonic stability theory, which posits that a single hegemonic state is both a necessary and sufficient condition for an open, liberal world economy. A change of hegemony in world politics is associated with global war.

Developers and advocates of hegemonic stability theory have been warning about the imminent threat of global war for decades. The late Susan Strange (1987, 552), founder of International Political Economy in Britain,

2   Introduction: the world falling apart

compared the myth of lost US hegemony to the once widely believed idea that German-speaking people came from a distinct Aryan race and to the persistent myth that rhinoceros horn is an aphrodisiac. Experts relying on false myths (see also Grunberg 1990), and driven by simple theories and ideologies, are usually not very good at predicting the future. Philip Tetlock's (2005, 20) systematic studies of expert anticipations of the future concludes:

> When we pit experts against minimalist performance benchmarks – dilettantes, dart-throwing chimps, and assorted extrapolation algorithms – we find few signs that expertise translates into greater ability to make either "well-calibrated" or "discriminating" forecasts.

A further problem with alarmism is that it can become a self-fulfilling prophecy. In the midst of everyday concerns and anxieties of life, the media-driven sense of things falling apart can breed socio-psychological mechanisms that generate existential insecurity, securitization of political issues and increasingly antagonistic self–other relations. Social systems are open, the future is conditionally responsive, so researchers must consider ethical and political responsibility.

Moreover, the world is contradictory. (Mega)trends can point in different directions. For instance, although the world economy has seen a long downward trend in the rates of investment and growth, and although inequalities, vulnerabilities and uncertainties have grown, economic reality remains complex. During the last four decades, the world population has grown from 4 to 7.5 billion, and the average world GDP per capita has at least doubled. Experience of the developments of the world economy are diverse and position and context specific.

The industrialization and rapid economic growth of China and India have led to the emergence of new strata of middle and upper class people.[3] Within overall growth, many parts of the world have experienced processes of deindustrialization – the former Soviet Union, North America, Latin America and many regions of Europe. Some poor and middle-income countries have stagnated or collapsed. Even in China, the share of manufacturing of GDP has been declining for decades. Thus, uneven growth and development generate complex and varied realities.

With these caveats in mind, this book argues that the possibility of global military catastrophe is real and increasingly likely (a global ecological catastrophe is equally likely, but not the focus of this book). This book can be read as a storm warning that would not make sense if it did not remain possible to avoid the worst of that storm. The storm analogy is of course partial. The storm I am talking about is a human-made geo-historical construction, not a natural phenomenon. But human-made historical constructions are also causally efficacious. Even if the worst-case scenario is not realized, the storm evoked by disintegrative tendencies in the global political economy will cause many troubles and crises.

The return of the past amidst relative stability

When anticipating the future, it is expedient to recall past forecasts and their failures. In the late twentieth century, the year 2000 was often seen as a decisive turning point. Many experts tried to foresee how things would look in the year 2000 and beyond (though a mythicized number 2000 does not have any bearing on relevant geo-historical processes). Johan Galtung (2000, 123), an eminent peace researcher and futurologist, explains that experts, many of them world-famous, were "remarkably wrong [about year 2000]; not only as a group but almost every single one of them".

Not everyone has been equally wrong. Hedley Bull, a British institutionalist International Relations scholar, stands out. In *The Anarchical Society*, Bull (1977) was right about the continued prevalence of the international society, constituted by shared rules, norms, understandings and institutions such as state sovereignty, diplomacy, international law, international organizations and great powerness. Underneath sensational media events and the daily drama of world politics, and despite some gradual changes and persisting potential for global catastrophe, the overall situation in 2017 appears mostly that of business as usual within international society. This is roughly in line with Bull's expectations.[4]

However, contra Bull, since the 1970s transnational organizations have proliferated. Bull seems to have underestimated globalizing forces (cf. Scholte 2005). Transnational corporations, banks and financial investors are now arguably more powerful (as noted early by Gill and Law 1989). New free trade and other international legal agreements have consolidated the privileged position of private megacorporations. Globalization may not be as new or discontinuous as sometimes depicted, but qualitatively novel features and properties have emerged: investment protection clauses, just-in-time systems of global production, digital derivatives markets, aggressive tax planning etc. Bull also neglected the possibility of the emergence of tentative elements of world statehood (cf. Albert et al. 2012; Albert 2016).

After the end of the Cold War, the world became more ideologically homogeneous. There were subsequent attempts to build systems of collective security, and even elements of world statehood – through human rights or economic treaties and in the functionally differentiated sphere of security (UN 1992). The relevant question now is: why has the world been reverting to nationalist statism, militarized conflicts and arms races, notwithstanding globalizing forces and the emergence of elements of global constitutionalism and security?

We can find some possible, albeit partial, answers, in Bull's account of international society. In the absence of consensus in the UN Security Council, the US and its NATO allies have resorted to unilateral wars of intervention. This raises issues of just war. As Bull (1977) noted, the problem with just war is that just causes can clash, whether in the public sphere or on the battleground (1977, 30, 132–3, 157–8). This has been the case in the Middle East, Central Asia and Ukraine. Bull also emphasized that attempts at collective security may weaken or undermine "classical devices for the maintenance of order" (1977, 231). If one great power can resort to war unilaterally, why not others?

The conflict between Putin's Russia and the West can be seen from this perspective: a likely consequence of unilateral attempts to execute collective security. This unilateralism has tacitly revived just war doctrine. For example, intervention in the Syrian civil war (2011–), has created potential for both cooperation and further escalation of antagonisms as "just" causes conflict. In Chapters 3 and 4, I discuss the problem of double standards and clashing interpretative perspectives in world politics. However, I also argue in this book that the dynamics of global political economy are key. The dynamic processes of the world economy shape conditions everywhere. Actors participate in bringing about and steering global political economy processes in various, but often short-sighted, counterproductive and contradictory ways (Patomäki 2008; Patomäki 2013).

The Bretton Woods system lasted from 1944 to 1973. The subsequent system has been characterized by a particular political project of globalization, where overall per capita rates of growth have gradually declined, though the world economy is still growing; inequalities have risen *within* most countries and in some ways between countries; the "normal" rate of unemployment has risen; and work has become increasingly precarious. The world economy has also been characterized by oscillations with increasing amplitude. Volatility has risen, especially in finance.[5] The financial crisis of 2008–2009 was the most serious crisis of the world economy since the 1930s and 1940s.[6] It almost produced a new great depression – the world economy verged on collapse – but automatic stabilizers, rescue and stimulus packages averted the worst. As Jonathan Kirshner (2014, 47) also argues, "the relatively benign international political environment in 2007–2008 compared with the intense security dilemma of the inter-war years were also essential in not making a bad situation worse".

Fallacy of composition (see Elster 1978, 97–106) is a key concept in this book. What is possible for one actor at a given moment is not possible for all or many simultaneously. This has collective policy implications.

Introduction: the world falling apart 5

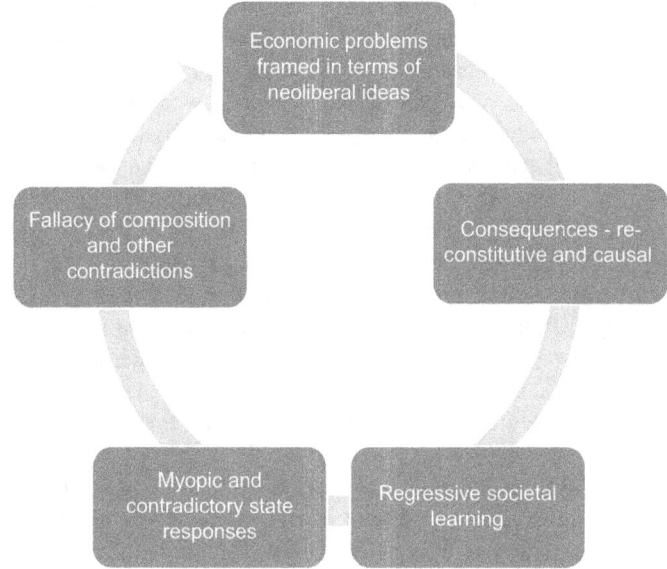

Figure 1.1 The self-reinforcing negative dynamics of the neoliberal world economy

For instance, any attempt to export a slump to other countries by reducing imports and increasing exports or by creating equivalent financial flows soon leads to a contradiction if everyone tries to do the same. The same applies to pursuing "competitiveness", whether it refers to exports or investment. For example, if the aim is to attract a maximal share of investment to maintain economic growth via corporate tax competition, there is no aggregate level historical evidence that this increases the overall pool of investment. Rather, the opposite seems to be true: investment rates have declined in the OECD as tax rates have fallen. If corporate tax cuts have a positive effect on the level of real investments in one country, it will likely do so at the expense of other countries. Short-sighted and contradictory ways of responding to problems of the world economy are both the cause and effect of problems (Figure 1.1).

The process tends to reinforce itself, partly because dynamics lead to political changes within and across states, often deepening and entrenching myopic self-regarding orientations. Many mechanisms can work toward this. For instance, volatile public opinion responds to changing conditions. Rising unemployment, widening social disparities and increasing uncertainty and dependence can generate existential insecurity among citizenry.[7] Economic problems tend to threaten identity, as not only one's earnings but also one's social worth, rights and duties are tied to a position as an employee, entrepreneur or capitalist. Economic problems can endanger social integration (Habermas 1988, 20–31). Given characteristic difficulties and pathologies of socialization in a complex market society, and related crises of embodied personality, the blend of capitalist world markets and separate national states involve great potential for antagonistic social relations.

These and related processes largely explain why the world has been reverting to nationalist statism, militarized conflicts and arms races. The international political environment is becoming less benign. An arms race too can follow from (i) responses to economic problems and (ii) a related fallacy of composition. For instance, a state may decide to stimulate its economy by spending more on armaments (i.e. resort to military Keynesianism) or keep a "security margin" by trying to be better armed than its actual or potential military adversaries. If all relevant states – or even just two of them – try the same, the result can be an arms race, which may escalate to war.[8]

The result of these dynamics is a gradual and partial return of the past. Sometimes this return may be ideologically explicit. Neoliberalism tends to evoke nineteenth-century economic liberalism and its values (see e.g. Hayek 1944, 240). In international economic relations, the dominance of policies of free trade and free movement of capital signify a return to types of regime that existed before World War I. The re-emergence of power-balancing practices – following the brief post–Cold War period of globalism and the peace dividend – is another sign of a re-formation of a pre-WWI system type. The historical analogy to pre-WWI world is only partial.[9] In some ways the 2010s resemble the late 1920s and early 1930s: faulty monetary design, financialization and debt-fuelled Ponzi growth led to a global financial crisis that begat deflationary forces which have strengthened a mix of racist nationalism and populism. Yanis Varoufakis has coined the term "postmodern 1930s", a concatenation that also stresses differences between eras and that invokes the idea that signs and symbols are taking primacy over tangible reality.[10]

Contents of the book

The goal of this book is to illuminate the causes of currently prevailing tendencies towards disintegration, antagonism and – ultimately – war. But I also try to show how these developments are embedded in deeper processes of human learning. Thus, I explore those world-historical mechanisms and processes that have (i) created the conditions for our current predicament while (ii) simultaneously involving the potential for better futures. I do so in the spirit of H. G. Wells, invoking his aphorism that "civilization is in a race between education and catastrophe". My objective is to further human learning in the current world-historical conjuncture, not to contribute to self-fulfilling prophecies.

In Chapter 2, I focus on disintegrative tendencies within the EU, itself an integral part of the world economy. As Brexit demonstrates, trust in the EU and its institutions, and in neoliberal globalization, has declined due to a prolonged economic downturn and series of crises, with deep roots in the financialization process. The social effects of and political responses to these relative economic developments must be understood in terms of prevailing standards and expectations. As the young Marx (1847) noted 170 years ago, "our desires and pleasures spring from society; we measure them, therefore, by society and not by the objects which serve for their satisfaction". Our wants and pleasures are relative to the general development of society.

The cosmopolitan left has been successful in elections in Greece and Spain – countries with recent historical experience of right-wing dictatorships – but for the most part rising discontent in Europe has been channelled into nationalist and disintegrative politics of othering and scapegoating. Right-wing nationalist–populist parties have become established in the legislatures of most European countries. In some cases, they have risen to government. On the left, Plan B and Lexit ("left exit") achieved greater popularity after Syriza's surrender (accepting the third EU Memorandum on Greece's debt, on terms set in Brussels, Frankfurt and Berlin).

Brexit is not a deterministic result of these dynamic developments. The global financial crisis did not hit the UK particularly hard in GDP or unemployment terms. The Euro crisis has affected the UK more indirectly than directly. To explain Brexit, we need to specify subtle and indirect connections and mechanisms. Nevertheless, the decision to exit the EU stemmed from grievances and protests not unique to the UK. Similar responses have occurred across the EU. There is a widespread perception that Europe is returning to its barbarous past. "Proud peoples are being turned against each other. Nationalism, extremism and racism are being re-awakened."[11] But it is not only Europe. Similar mechanisms and tendencies are in effect across the world, as is evident from the prominence of nationalist–populist political leaders – Recep Tayyip Erdoğan, Vladimir Putin, Donald Trump etc.

Chapter 2 is thus not only about Brexit. In it I outline some of the chief explanatory ideas of the book: there are internal and external relations between neoliberalism and nationalism; a causal process flows from economic troubles to resentment and emotional distancing; and Karl Polanyi's double movement that starts with the construction of self-regulating markets and results in societal self-protection. My analysis of Brexit and, more generally, disintegrative tendencies in the EU, is a first step towards understanding the dynamics of the whole global political economy. I conclude Chapter 2 by providing a tentative explanation of why UKIP's apparently paradoxical espousal of free markets is currently quite typical.

In Chapter 3, I examine the conflict in Ukraine in order to understand and explain why the world is reverting to nationalist statism and territorial conflicts. I make three arguments. First, and most importantly, the EU has played an active role in various global processes that have co-created the conditions for a new Russia–West conflict and the war in Ukraine. The EU promotes free markets, austerity and various neoliberal measures, and their effects aggravate social conflicts. I explain how the relevant mechanisms work and how their effects involve positive feedback loops and cumulative causation. Global Keynesian institutions and policies would be needed to counter these and other related tendencies. Secondly, while Russia exemplifies tendencies toward past practices of power-balancing, the self-righteous universalism of the EU and US is also liable to create division. Normatively I argue that new institutional frameworks of dialogue, cooperation and democratic participation could transcend the conflict of perspectives and principles.

In Chapter 4, I examine the causes and consequences of Donald Trump's presidency. The rise of China and other BRICS and Asian countries, and the relocation of industry to nearby countries, has hastened deindustrialization in many parts of Europe and North America. Combined with other characteristic effects of prevailing policies and globalization, especially rising inequalities, deindustrialization has fuelled political turmoil in the US, resulting in the election of Trump. The exercise of double standards within as well as by the US, and the dogged pursuit of its own national sovereignty and narrow "national interests", contradicts and tends to undermine the course of international cooperation and thus destabilize the world economy (when a country is or is not applying double standards is of course open to conflicting interpretations).

The irony in this historical situation is that the US appears, both now and in the past, to assume that others will nevertheless continue to abide by agreed rules, norms and principles, though often it does not do so itself. Future scenarios of global change will now largely pivot on how others respond to changes in US attitudes and actions. Will the US continue to act uncooperatively internationally, and single-mindedly pursue its vision of strengthened "national sovereignty" (at home and abroad)? The consequences of such a course are likely to be disruptive, not only for the formal sphere of international cooperation and prospects for future global governance, but for the global economic system as well. A spiral of aggressive actions and retaliatory reactions could be set in motion. The probable long-term consequences of such a pattern are well known, as any reading of the first half of the twentieth century reveals (e.g. Moser 2016).

I distinguish between four relevant scenarios about the possible and likely effects of Trumponomics, especially in trade and investments. Trade protectionism via tariffs or complicated arrangements of taxation are not the only forms of potential beggar-thy-neighbour policies. Attempts to enhance external competitiveness by internal devaluation or tax competition can be equally harmful. Some countries, and the EU, are keen to increase their competitiveness. The idea is to increase demand for national goods and services in world markets – at the expense of other countries. Yet the return of classical trade protectionism would be another step toward repeating the 1930s.

Overall the effect of the Trump administration is to aggravate and intensify the pathologies and contradictions of the world political economy. Tax reductions for US corporations, middle classes and the very wealthy, and increasing infrastructure and military spending, are neither sustainable nor generalizable under the prevailing global institutional setting. The Trump administration is also proposing potentially far-reaching financial deregulation. The stated aim is to make US financial companies more competitive – but in all likelihood at the expense of global financial stability. The Trump administration's financial deregulation policy seems determined to speed up the financial boom-and-bust process; if successful, an early massive financial crisis is more likely. The effects of financial deregulation, combined with other aspects of US political developments such as the decline of the rule of law, may also have the unintended consequence of decreasing the attractiveness of the US economy as a global economic "safe-haven".

In Chapter 5, I discuss the explosive potential of the state system and the capitalist world economy in more general terms. The self-reinforcing negative dynamics of the contemporary world economy bring about context-specific outcomes that, in spite of their differences, share essential characteristics. Variations of similar developments can be observed across the world: in the EU and its member states such as Hungary, Poland and Britain, in the US, Russia, Ukraine, Turkey, China and India. These outcomes are internally and externally related to changes in economic growth, profit, employment, wages, taxes, income distribution and welfare, which are dependent on economic policies and institutional and regulatory arrangements. From a Keynesian–Kaleckian economic-theoretical perspective, once orthodox economic-liberal policies and institutions are dominant, they tend to slow down economic growth through various mechanisms. Positive feedback loops dominate, which tend to make growth uneven and increase disparities between regions and social classes and strata.

Increasing inequality is an important reason why legitimacy may be lacking and why overall demand in the world economy tends to be insufficient. One of the key claims of Piketty's (2014) *Capital* is the tendency for r > g, where r is the average annual rate of return on capital and g is annual economic growth. This is especially likely when growth is slow. Past wealth becomes increasingly important and inherited wealth grows faster than output and income. Piketty states that "we can now see those shocks [world wars] as the only forces since the Industrial Revolution powerful enough to reduce inequality" (8; italics HP). In Chapter 5, I argue that Piketty is not fully consistent in formulating this point. Developments are much more contingent and open-systemic than Piketty allows. Nonetheless, if there is a close relationship between wars, lack of growth and inequalities, must we then wait for the next global war before inequalities reduce or are peaceful changes possible? It seems the global financial crisis 2008–2009 was not compelling enough. Perhaps a more devastating economic and political shock is required for real changes to become possible. What kind of crisis or shock could push world history onto a new path?

I also reverse this question in Chapter 5. What will the concentration of capital and the rising importance of past and inherited wealth mean to the likelihood of a major economic and political disaster? Piketty maintains that the developments we are now observing are likely to erode democracy. Are these high levels of inequalities incompatible with democracy per se? What are the consequences of de-democratization and how are they connected to the rise of nationalist populism?

My starting point in the concluding Chapter 6 is that doctrines codify the lessons learned from previous practices; and doctrinal debates define geo-historical eras and their characteristic practical and institutional arrangements. Collective learning and the exercise of power (understood as transformative capacity), not least by social movements, determine which doctrines prevail. The idea of a neoliberal world order is contested. The historical outcome of this global contestation, both ideologically and practically, will turn upon how states and social forces around the world act and respond in the coming period. This outcome is historically indeterminate; reality involves complex multi-path developmental processes.

In Chapter 6, I make a case for the importance of holoreflexivity. Holoreflexivity means that one can see oneself as an active part of a dynamic whole. "It is global in that it encompasses all social groupings, communities, cultures and civilizations, and planetary in that it comprises the totality of relationships between the human species and the rest of the biosphere."[12] A rational *holoreflexive* response to the consequence of the new liberal orthodoxy would be to extend the spatial scale of

Keynesian-Kaleckian and related alternatives, and re-articulate them in global-democratic terms.

In the concluding chapter, I draw different threads of my argument together by discussing scenarios *concerning* the dynamics of the EU and of the whole world economy. It is increasingly probable that the transformation and metamorphosis of the systems of global governance will come about via a series of deep crises, possibly ending in a major global catastrophe. Yet there is also a rational tendential direction to world history, more firmly based than any history of contingent events. The rational tendential direction is grounded in collective human learning.

Any claim about rational tendential direction of world history has to be understood as a dialectical argument within the meaningful human sphere. These arguments are practical. Transformations toward a rational tendential direction is not automatic, it is realized through transformative praxis, a contingent process which is in turn dependent upon the rationality of participating individual actors. The minimal meaning of rationality is openness to reason and learning. Once context-specific learning has occurred and a reasonable direction set, the next logical step is the process of constructing transformative agency. This could assume, for instance, the form of a global political party.

The questions I am posing in this book are ultimately about the future of capitalist world economy. The processes of transformation may involve many surprises. The future is uncertain, in part because creativity and novelty are unpredictable. This is what makes world history so fascinating even in a context of grave dangers.

Notes

1 Ample evidence suggests that overall violence and war in human society has been declining for centuries (notably violent deaths per annum relative to population; see Elias ([1939] 1978); Gurr (1981); Pinker (2011); and Muchembled (2012).
2 See Global Terrorism Database (www.start.umd.edu/gtd/). Most incidents of terrorism during the past 15 years have occurred in Iraq and other conflict zones. In Western Europe and North America, terrorism is statistically rare. See Nowrasteh (2016) for a US-based risk analysis. For Western Europe, see www.datagraver.com/case/people-killed-by-terrorism-per-year-in-western-europe-1970-2015.
3 European colonization led to a fall in Asian manufacturing and global output share, affecting mainly India, China and South East Asia. A part of the story of the neoliberal era is that these eighteenth- to twentieth-century developments have reversed. Moreover, wages of Chinese or Indian labourers working in export industries are increasing, and where social insurance systems operate, global inequalities are mitigated in aggregate. It remains true that overall the last three decades have been dominated by an exacerbation of inequalities (in terms

of income, social protection, access to higher education and fulfilling jobs, and humanizing living conditions).
4 See Patomäki (2017). Note most IR scholars, including Bull, did not anticipate the end of the Cold War; Deutsch (1954) is a rare exception (see Allan and Goldmann 1992, including Patomäki 1992b, for an *ex post* evaluation of IR theories in this light). Moreover, for a decade after the end of the Cold War it seemed that the practice of power-balancing was disappearing, at least on a global scale.
5 For discussion and explanation of the world economy before the global financial crisis of 2008–2009, see Patomäki (2008, ch 5). Since then per capita economic growth has reduced further both in the OECD and many other parts of the world.
6 For an explanation of the crisis, see e.g. Minsky (2008); Patomäki (2010); Rasmus (2010); and Galbraith (2014).
7 Many scholars start from Anthony Giddens: "In respect of feelings of ontological security, the members of modern societies are particularly vulnerable to generalized anxiety. This may become intense either when, as individuals, they have to confront existential dilemmas ordinarily suppressed by sequestration, or when, on a larger scale, routines of social life are for some reason substantially disrupted. The emptiness of the routines followed in large segments of modern social life engender a psychological basis for affiliation to symbols that can both promote solidarity and cause schism. Among these symbols are those associated with nationalism" (Giddens 1985, 196–7). Another possibility is provided by the texts and symbols of religion where responses vary from deeply reflexive Kierkegaardian existential faith (Krishek and Furtak 2011) to modern fundamentalism, including political Christianity and Islam (Ruthven 2007).
8 For Richardson's explosive arms race model, where parties seek a "security margin", see Rapoport (1960, 15–30). Robert Jervis's (1976, 62–82 *et passim*) Spiral Model is more sophisticated, since it explicitly incorporates misperceptions, self-fulfilling prophecies, lessons drawn from history etc.
9 In historical analogy, there are both horizontal and vertical relations. Horizontal relations concern similarities and differences between eras at the level of actual events, trends and developments, while vertical relations concern relevant causal mechanisms and processes within them (as well as possible causal connections between them). All historical analogies are partial; and vertical relations are usually more important than horizontal. A key historical analogy of my book *The Political Economy of Global Security* (Patomäki 2008) is that the contemporary era is in some important regards similar to the era of 1870–1914. In that book, I focused on vertical relations of analogy and pointed out that there are also some dissimilar or partly novel mechanisms. On this basis, and via related analysis of layers of agency, structures and mechanisms, I constructed three scenarios of possible global futures, with variations in each. Over the past ten years, the world seems to have followed scenario one, where a long downturn and uneven growth persist in the world economy. In the context of neo-territorialized and at times neo-imperial competition between super-states and blocs, the dynamics of the system lead to securitization, enemy-construction, new alliances and an arms race.
10 E.g. Varoufakis (2016). Freinacht (2017) argues plausibly that "this comparison [to the 1930s] has its merits, but it's not without dangers of becoming too anachronistic if our allegories are taken too literally and if we fail to include a sound analysis of the present. It's important to keep in mind that we're living in a vastly different world than our close ancestors a century ago. So even if some of the

Introduction: the world falling apart 13

mechanisms and patterns seem to be similar, the outcomes are likely to be very different."
11 A Manifesto for Democratising Europe, drafted by Yanis Varoufakis, available: https://blogs.mediapart.fr/edition/les-invites-de-mediapart/article/040216/yanis-varoufakis-manifesto-democratising-europe.
12 Camilleri and Falk (2009, 537).

References

Albert, Mathias. 2016. *A Theory of World Politics*. Cambridge Studies in International Relations. Cambridge: Cambridge University Press.
Albert, Mathias, Gorm Harste, Heikki Patomäki, and Knud-Erik Jørgensen. 2012. "Introduction: World State Futures." *Cooperation and Conflict* 47 (2): 145–56.
Allan, Pierre, and Kjell Goldmann, eds. 1992. *The End of the Cold War: Evaluating Theories of International Relations*. Dordrecht: Martinus Nijhoff.
Belluz, Julia. 2016. "You May Think the World Is Falling Apart: Steven Pinker Is Here to Tell You It Isn't." Steven Pinker's interview, *Vox*, September 10. www.vox.com/2016/8/16/12486586/2016-worst-year-ever-violence-trump-terrorism.
Bull, Hedley. 1977. *The Anarchical Society: A Study of Order in World Politics*. London: Macmillan.
Camilleri, Joseph A., and Jim Falk. 2009. *Worlds in Transition: Evolving Governance across a Stressed Planet*. Northampton: Edward Elgar.
Elias, Norbert. (1939) 1978. *The Civilizing Process: The History of Manners*. Translated by Edmund Jephcott. New York: Urizen Books.
Elster, Jon. 1978. *Logic and Society: Contradictions and Possible Worlds*. Chichester: John Wiley & Sons.
Freinacht, Hanzi. 2017. "Welcome to the Postmodern 1930s." *Metamoderna*, February 26. http://metamoderna.org/welcome-to-the-postmodern-1930s?lang=en.
Galbraith, James K. 2014. *The End of Normal: The Great Crisis and the Future of Growth*. New York: Simon & Schuster.
Galtung, Johan. 2000. "What Did People Predict for the Year 2000 and What Happened?" *Futures* 35 (2): 123–45.
Giddens, Anthony. 1985. *The Nation-State and Violence: Volume Two of a Contemporary Critique of Historical Materialism*. Cambridge: Polity Press.
Gill, Stephen R., and David Law. 1989. "Global Hegemony and the Structural Power of Capital." *International Studies Quarterly* 33 (4): 475–99.
Grunberg, Isabelle. 1990. "Exploring the 'Myth' of Hegemonic Stability." *International Organization* 44 (4): 431–77.
Gurr, Ted R. 1981. "Historical Trends in Violent Crime: Europe and the United States." *Crime and Justice: An Annual Review of Research* 3 (1): 295–350.
Habermas, Jürgen. 1988. *Legitimation Crisis*. Translated by Thomas McCarthy. Cambridge: Polity Press.
Hayek, Friedrich. 1944. *The Road to Serfdom*. Chicago: University of Chicago Press.
Jervis, Robert. 1976. *Perception and Misperception in International Politics*. Princeton: Princeton University Press.

14 Introduction: the world falling apart

Kirshner, Jonathan. 2014. "International Relations Then and Now: Why the Great Recession Was Not the Great Depression." *History of Economic Ideas* 22 (3): 47–69.

Krishek, Sharon, and Rick Anthony Furtak. 2011. "A Cure for Worry? Kierkegaardian Faith and the Insecurity of Human Existence." *International Journal for Philosophy of Religion* 72 (3): 157–75.

Marx, Karl. 1847. "Wage Labour and Capital." Edited and translated by Friedrich Engels. First Published (in German): *Neue Rheinische Zeitung*, Nos. 264–267 and 269, April 5–8 and 11, 1849. Online Version: Marx/Engels Internet Archive (marxists.org) 1993, 1999. www.marxists.org/archive/marx/works/download/Marx_Wage_Labour_and_Capital.pdf.

Minsky, Hyman. 2008. *Stabilizing an Unstable Economy*. New York: McGraw-Hill.

Moser, John E. 2016. *Global Great Depression and the Coming of World War II*. London: Routledge.

Muchembled, Robert. 2012. *A History of Violence: From the End of Middle Ages to the Present*. Translated by Jean Birrell. Cambridge: Polity Press.

Nowrasteh, Alex. 2016. "Terrorism and Immigration." *Cato Institute Policy Analysis*, no. 798, September 13. https://object.cato.org/sites/cato.org/files/pubs/pdf/pa798_1_1.pdf.

Patomäki, Heikki. 1992a. "From Normative Utopias to Political Dialectics: Beyond a Deconstruction of the Brown-Hoffman Debate." *Millennium: Journal of International Studies* 21 (1): 53–75.

Patomäki, Heikki. 1992b. "What Is It That Changed with the End of the Cold War? An Analysis of the Problem of Identifying and Explaining Change." In *The End of the Cold War: Evaluating Theories of International Relations*, edited by Pierre Allan and Kjell Goldmann, 179–225. Dordrecht: Martinus Nijhoff.

Patomäki, Heikki. 2008. *Political Economy of Global Security: War, Future Crises and Changes of Global Governance*. Rethinking Globalizations. London: Routledge.

Patomäki, Heikki. 2010. "What Next? An Explanation of the 2008–2009 Slump and Two Scenarios of the Shape of Things to Come." *Globalizations* 7 (1): 67–84.

Patomäki, Heikki. 2013. *The Great Eurozone Disaster: From Crisis to Global New Deal*. Economic Controversies. London: Zed Books.

Patomäki, Heikki. 2017. "Review of *Capitalism: Competition, Conflict, Crisis*, by Anwar Shaikh." *Journal of Critical Realism*, first published online June 1, 2017. doi: http://dx.doi.org/10.1080/14767430.2017.1332807.

Piketty, Thomas. 2014. *Capital in the Twenty-First Century*. Translated by Arthur Goldhammer. Cambridge: The Belknap Press (of Harvard University Press).

Pinker, Steven. 2011. *The Better Angels of Our Nature: The Decline of Violence in History and Its Causes*. London: Allen Lane.

Rapoport, Anatol. 1960. *Fights, Games and Debates*. Ann Arbor: University of Michigan Press.

Rasmus, Jack. 2010. *Epic Recession: Prelude to Global Depression*. London: Pluto Press.

Ruthven, Malise. 2007. *Fundamentalism: A Very Short Introduction*. Oxford: Oxford University Press.

Scholte, Jan Aart. 2005. *Globalization: A Critical Introduction*. 2nd revised and updated ed. Basingstoke: Palgrave Macmillan.
Strange, Susan. 1987. "The Persistent Myth of Lost Hegemony." *International Organization* 41 (4): 551–74.
Tetlock, Philip E. 2005. *Expert Political Judgement*. Princeton: Princeton University Press.
UN (United Nations) General Assembly. 1992. *An Agenda for Peace: Preventive Diplomacy, Peacemaking and Peace-Keeping*. A/47/277-S/24111. www.un.org/ruleoflaw/files/A_47_277.pdf.
Varoufakis, Yanis. 2016. "Trump Victory Comes with a Silver Lining for the World's Progressives." *The Conversation*, November 11. https://theconversation.com/trump-victory-comes-with-a-silver-lining-for-the-worlds-progressives-68523.

2 Brexit and the causes of European disintegration

Brexit is an earth-shattering moment in the history of European integration. Until summer 2016, integration and enlargement followed each other. With Brexit, this process is being reversed, creating negative future expectations. Is this the beginning of the end? Has the EU become irreparable? Is the disintegration of Yugoslavia being repeated on the scale of the EU (Becker 2017)?

Events involve duration and some change. Momentous events have always been the bread and butter of narrative history (Sewell 1996). Prime Minister David Cameron's decision to hold an EU membership referendum started a process that led to June 2016. This was based on a miscalculation. Prior to formal election campaigning in January 2013, Cameron pledged to hold an in/out referendum if the Conservatives won a majority in 2015. Received wisdom before the election was that there would be another coalition government, and that a Liberal Democrat Party partner would reject a referendum; thus, centrist Conservatives could make the pledge, benefit from it and likely never need to implement it.

Cameron's intent seems to have been to both undercut the growing popularity of the UK Independence Party (UKIP) and silence Conservative Euro-sceptics. European integration has been a long-term source of division within the Conservative Party. Unintended consequences, however, dominated the process. The immediate effect of a referendum pledge was to focus debate on immigration. This debate provided a degree of legitimacy to UKIP and a point of convergence for Conservative sceptics. UKIP increased their vote from less than 1 million to 3.8 million in the 2015 general election. Essentially, Cameron contributed to shifting the Overton Window – the range of ideas that are acceptable to the public and assume centre stage in political discourse – accommodating the sceptics and UKIP's way of positioning a much broader set of issues.[1] This shift affected the outcome of the relatively tight referendum in June 2016.

It is important, however, to take a wider, longer-term view of the causes of Brexit. Events and episodes occur within geo-historical processes. Several processes may occur simultaneously and coalesce and interact in various ways. Together they constitute the context of actions, including background (practical skills), practical and institutional rules and political and economic circumstances. Reasons for and rationalizations of actions are related to these deeper and wider processes in complicated ways. The underlying processes may, for instance, provide grounds for accusation or excuses. It is easy to criticize Cameron for his opportunistic miscalculation, but he could plausibly cite the political context and expectations that were common in 2013–2015. Interpretations of the underlying processes are part of political processes themselves.

There are many possible ways to study underlying processes. The first is to move deeper into discursive formations and meanings: for instance, explicating the meaning structures underpinning a political stand in relation to the EU. For example, why is it that in Germany and France "Europe" usually means "us", but in the UK it tends to mean "them"? Perhaps Brexit could be partly explained in terms of an absence of a British World War narrative that would justify deep involvement in the European integration process (Reynolds 2017); or in terms of the ambiguities of post-imperial "Britishness" and related identity-political manoeuvrings occurring in different parts of the UK (Gardner 2017).

Another way to move deeper is to explain the contextual and relational possibilities open to a positioned actor. A good example is Cameron's apparent opportunity to increase his party's popularity by calling for a referendum. This opportunity was made possible by the underlying institutions and their rules (such as parliamentary democracy, voting system, laws concerning referenda, article 50 of the Lisbon Treaty etc). Cameron decided to seize this opportunity in response to specific geo-historical circumstances. The relevant circumstances included the rise of UKIP and related ideas across parties, but also dispute concerning the significance of the City of London. As a strategic political actor, Cameron was playing a two-level game (Putnam 1988). In domestic politics, he was trying to win elections, and in the EU, he was seeking further concessions to the UK.

Identity politics and the two-level game do not suffice to explain why anti-EU and anti-immigration sentiments were growing stronger, why UKIP was gaining in popularity and why 52% of the active voters eventually preferred "Leave" in June 2016. Voters across Europe have rejected the EU several times in the past. Many specific EU treaties have been overruled in national referenda, even within the original EEC6 (in France and Holland). Norway has rejected EU membership twice. If the order of the 1994 referenda in

18 *Brexit and the causes of European disintegration*

the Nordic countries had been different, at least Sweden would have stayed out and perhaps Finland. The number of UK voters supporting staying in the EU was roughly the same in 2016 as it was in 1975 (16,141,241 and 17,378,581, respectively). Population growth and higher turnout enabled the "leave" side to get twice as many votes in 2016 than it did in 1975. It should also be borne in mind that many nationalist right-wing parties in Europe have relatively long historical roots. The Austrian Freedom Party was founded in 1956 and the French National Front in 1972. Most of the parties with a substantial number of seats in a national parliament in 2017 emerged between the late 1980s and early 2000s.

The 2016 UK referendum was a break from past patterns. For the first time, a member state decided to leave the Union. Even those focussing on identity politics admit that economic inequalities arising from globalization were another major factor in the referendum (Gardner 2017, 10). Many observers have pointed out that it was broader working and lower social classes who voted leave, rather than just the nationalist right or those representing business interests. "The division of the Brexit vote does not coincide with racial or gender differences, but to a large extent reflects the difference in class" (Kagarlitsky 2017, 111). Yet many of those belonging, in this interpretation, to the working class are no longer blue collar workers, and cumulative immigration of visible others was real in the UK (its meaning was of course negatively shaped by Leave campaigners). The "Leave" vote was especially popular in deindustrialized areas of England "with GDP per capita less than half inner London levels, and now hardest hit by cutbacks in services" (Watkins 2016, 23). What seems to have emerged is a temporary constellation of forces in which Conservative sceptics, long-term UKIP activists and lower strata or peripheral parts of society – hit hard by the consequences of neoliberalism, globalization and deindustrialization – converged around the referendum.

The emergence of this constellation of forces is in no way unique to the UK. Similar developments have been occurring across Europe (and globally; see later chapters). The politico-economic elite has been wavering regarding nationalism and the EU and global governance, perhaps partly in response to a slight shift among political forces toward social democratic multilateralism (Harmes 2012). Increasing inequalities between social classes and regions, and underlying political economy processes such as deindustrialization, have generated a rise of anti-elite populism in the UK and elsewhere. We would thus need to explain the characteristic outcomes of prevailing political economy processes and how they are connected to attempts to protect society, particularly against outsiders. Moreover, the task is also to explain how anti-elite protest and nationalist protectionism can converge, at least temporarily, with Conservative EU-scepticism, libertarianism and global free market and trade policies. A paradox lies at the heart of the causal complex that generates disintegrative tendencies.

The utopia of free markets and alternatives to it in European politics

Margaret Thatcher's appointment as British prime minister in 1979, followed by Ronald Reagan's presidency in the US, marked the beginning of the neoliberal era. Neoliberalism is a programme of resolving problems of, and developing, human society by means of competitive markets. Things and processes can be identified as problems only within a framework, and neoliberal theories frame things and processes (for example, moderately high inflation in the 1960s and 1970s, and competitiveness of states, emerged as key problems). Competitive markets are assumed to be efficient and just and to maximize freedom of choice. Competitive markets can be private and actual, or they can be simulated within organizations, whether private or public. Market-like incentive structures within organizations are fully compatible with steep hierarchies and characteristically require extensive systems of surveillance and auditing. Neoliberalism is comprised of theories that are in some ways contradictory, all of which can be developed in different directions; and yet all these theories posit competitive markets as superior in terms of efficiency, justice or freedom, or a combination of these (Patomäki 2009).

The new economic liberalism advocating free trade, open markets, privatization, deregulation and reducing the size of the public sector spread rapidly across the world. It was strongly favoured by the structural discrepancy between territorial states and the global economy and the consequent asymmetries of power (Patomäki 2008, 130–45); it was also supported by the US and British political domination of the World Bank, the International Monetary Fund (IMF) and, later, the OECD and GATT, the precursor to the World Trade Organization. Neoliberalism was also to have a decisive impact on the process that led to the Maastricht Treaty that formally established the European Union, replacing the European Community 1 November 1993. The European Central Bank (ECB) was built on monetarist principles propounded by Milton Friedman and like-minded neoclassical economists, who also influenced Thatcher.[2] The EU is essentially a single market with no corresponding state structures.

It would thus seem that differences between British and EU versions of neoliberalism are limited. The dynamics of swings in public opinion in the UK and elsewhere are subtle and complex. Consider the four non-exhaustive but typical possibilities presented in Table 2.1. Support for the EU, or criticism of it, does not stem self-evidently from any of the four options. In

20 *Brexit and the causes of European disintegration*

Table 2.1 Four ethico-political alternatives in European politics

	Left-orientation (cooperation, solidarity; freedom and efficiency require socio-economic equality)	Market right-orientation (competition, private markets; freedom and efficiency require socio-economic differences)
National orientation ("we" = ethnic nation or citizens of a sovereign state)	National welfare state and democracy	National determination of policies and inclusion/ exclusion
Cosmopolitan orientation ("we" = humanity or world citizens)	Global Keynesianism, global social justice and/ or global democracy	Global free markets and movements, coupled with common institutions such as global money

terms of left–right division, the EU is widely and plausibly perceived to be mainly a right-wing neoliberal project, yet many on the left and right anticipate that this can change. The prevailing perceptions and anticipations have themselves been changing. For instance, in the UK, Thatcher's Conservative party at times supported, rejected/resisted and sought to shape the European integration process. It has been acceptable in so far as it has fostered market-freedoms, and in so far as there has been a perception that it can become more free-private-market oriented in the future (justifying some ceding of sovereignty).

However, by the time David Cameron became leader, the Euro-sceptic right of the party were becoming increasingly restive and the party more ambivalent. This may have been partly because, in the aftermath of the global financial crisis of 2008–2009, the EU Commission started to advocate financial taxes and stronger regulation of finance (in 2016 the City of London nonetheless mainly supported "Remain" to avoid uncertainty and threats to its role). Another shift, from left to right, concerns the nationalist–populist parties. In their anti-establishment rhetoric, these parties have at times defended nationally based welfare-systems for native citizens; but when positioned to make decisions, they have characteristically consented to neo- or ordo-liberal policies (from option A to B in Table 2.1). On the left, in turn, the popularity of Plan B and Lexit rose rapidly after the dramatic surrender of Syriza in summer 2015. The Plan B manifesto was signed in late 2015 by many of Europe's best-known Left politicians, including Oskar Lafointane and Yanis Varoufakis, but soon experienced splits between nationalists and cosmopolitans.

Shifts over national/cosmopolitan and left/right divides are dynamic and complex. In their orientation, both the neoliberals and their post-Keynesian critics can be either national or cosmopolitan.³ In countries considering entering the EU, the cosmopolitan left has been divided, commonly arguing and voting against joining the EU. Once in, they have shifted position and declared that the EU must be must be transformed, because developments are path-dependent, and cosmopolitanism can be furthered through the EU. Some cosmopolitans on the right, such as Robert Mundell, have been enthusiastic about the EU, but consistent formulations of free market globalism are rare. Usually global economic liberalism has been premised (i) on the free movement of goods, services and capital and (ii) on national powers to limit the movements of people. The capitalist world economy is also about exclusion.

Since the formation of the Maastricht Treaty, but especially as a response to the flow of crises that started 2008–2009, the overall effects have amounted to diffusion of doubts about, and distrust in, the European integration project. To understand the complex dynamics of various shifts, we need theory-derived but falsifiable hypotheses to explain why the overall trend has been towards renationalization of politics (the main tendency) and towards the cosmopolitan left's transformative ideas (a weaker tendency, so far having involved significant electoral success mainly in Greece and Spain). The UK 2017 general election was about the EU, or about governance of the world economy, only indirectly.

Real–world politico-economic developments in the UK

When Thatcher was elected 1979, manufacturing accounted for almost 30% of Britain's national income and employed 6.8 million people; by 2016, it accounted for just 10% of national income and employed 2.7 million.⁴ The British economy has become increasingly financialized and dependent on the banking sector and the City of London. Most new jobs have emerged in the service sector. British GDP grew from the early or mid-1980s until the global financial crisis of 2008–2009, with the exception of the currency crisis and slump of the early 1990s. GDP growth came to a halt in 2008–2009. Income inequalities in the UK rose until the early 2000s and have remained at a relatively high level since then. The wealthy parts of Greater London, the South East region and the thriving parts of urban areas elsewhere prospered, while many rural areas and former industrial sites across the country were impoverished.⁵

Highly financialized EU economies such as the UK and Ireland were instantly hit by the global financial crisis. Since then British economic development has stagnated. There has been little per capita GDP growth in a decade. Despite some recovery in 2016, average working-age household incomes have remained below the level of 2007.[6] Deindustrialization and uneven regional development have continued. Early in the crisis a New Labour UK government re-stabilized the banking sector. Since then, the Cameron government and its successor has maintained preferential treatment of banking and pursued austerity policies (albeit at varying rates). Measures have included increasing VAT to 20%, a wide range of cuts to the benefit system and to housing benefit and mortgage interest relief. There have been significant increases in the cost of meeting basic needs such as utilities and housing. The Conservative government has implemented the heaviest cuts at local government level. Between 2009–2010 and 2014–2015 spending by England's local authorities was cut by a fifth and further cuts were scheduled for 2015–2020. The most deprived English councils suffered the biggest cuts in spending power. As a result, local and regional differences have intensified. As a rule, this worsened the conditions of those living in the deindustrialized areas prior to Brexit.[7]

For three decades, the benefits of GDP growth have flowed primarily to already prosperous regions, parts of cities and upper social strata. This stratification is also evident between urban and more rural or deindustrialized settings. Many households have resorted to debt to meet costs of living and to maintain consumption in line with societal expectations. Moreover, GDP growth has become ambiguous from the point of view of qualitative measures of life satisfaction or sustainable well-being. It is true that from 1993 to 2007, GPI per capita also rose in the UK, indicating a rise in real welfare, but this period was accompanied by continuous deindustrialization and characterized by persistent inequalities, vulnerabilities and insecurity.[8] The downturn that started with the global financial crisis (Rasmus 2010), and then continued as the Euro crisis (Patomäki 2013, ch 4) and UK austerity policies, has exacerbated debt problems and contributed to localized unemployment, and transitions to precarious employment. In combination, the prospects and well-being of large groups and segments of people were further weakened or made more uncertain.

What matters is not only socio-economic conditions but how they are perceived and interpreted relative to people's social standing. Men who would once have been secure in a long-term industry-related identity now feel demeaned in precarious job markets. A case study of impoverished post-industrial Doncaster reveals how the lack of job security and decline of both social rights and trade unions have contributed to heightened existential insecurity among the citizenry (Thorleifsson 2016). The aftermath of the financial crisis brought with it not only austerity policy but also rhetorical attempts to victimize victims and marginalize the many. Philosopher Michael Sandel (in Cowley 2016) explains how the dignity of many people has "been eroded and mocked by developments with globalization,

Brexit and the causes of European disintegration 23

the rise of finance, the attention that is lavished by parties across the political spectrum on economic and financial elites, the technocratic emphasis of the established political parties". Immigration adds to the volatile mixture. Particularly during times of heightened existential insecurity, nostalgia and related turns to nationalism or religion can function as a potent source of meaning, identity and social reconnection.

The mechanisms and schemes translating changing economic circumstances into ethico-political responses

Figure 2.1 provides a schematic of the effects of globalization, neoliberal policies, automation and sudden economic changes or crises on the development of conservative, backward-looking and exclusionary beliefs and values. These processual mechanisms may affect only some of those belonging to the vulnerable parts of the population. Spontaneous articulation of emotional responses and related reasoning about the validity of a rule involve a limited number of (self-)selected individuals and groups. The overall formation of public opinion is complex, multi-layered and reflexive (Patomäki 1997). In large-scale modern societies, many actors are indifferent, ignorant, hypocritical or egoistically calculative, but a political rule is unstable without good normative reasons, considered important by a sufficient proportion of citizens and political actors (e.g. Sayer 2016). Changes in the framing of questions alter the percentage distribution of answers. At the same time, actors form opinions in relation to, and in terms of, public opinion. Public opinion is thus a context-sensitive, relational and reflexive phenomenon. Public opinion is also made to speak in the name of "the people", "common people", "silent majority", "mainstream" etc. Public opinion

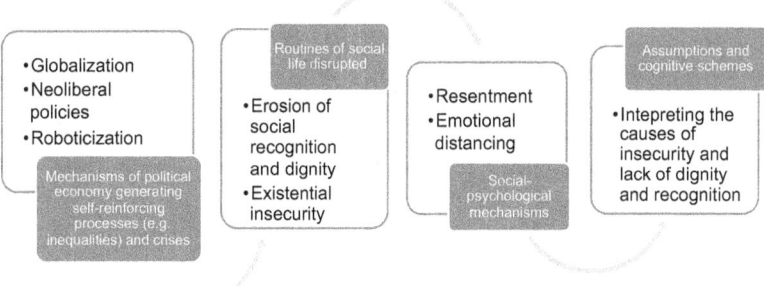

Figure 2.1 Politico-economic developments, social-psychological mechanisms and cognitive schemes

can be constitutive of social realities; it can authorize particular actions and practices. Even a limited first-order impact on opinions and sentiments can thus suffice to shift overall public opinion, especially when overall learning- and power-dynamics resonate with that shift.

In the 1990s the authors of Eurobarometers stressed that most EU-Europeans feel, and indeed often are, badly informed about most EU issues (e.g. Eurobarometer 1996, 56). The situation has not changed significantly since the 1990s. Eurobarometers test citizens' knowledge. It is commonly acknowledged that Britons are among the least knowledgeable about the EU (e.g. Hix 2015). Ignorance can make actors particularly open to influences and susceptible to the manipulation of meanings. An unstable public opinion can nonetheless exhibit continuities. Since the time of the Maastricht Treaty, many of the arguments pro and con the EU have remained the same. The EU has been legitimized in terms of peace in Europe, performance of technical-functional tasks and the benefits of a single market and currency. Public debates have revolved around economistic calculations of costs and benefits of the EU to the individual, business or nation; around fears about "our country losing its identity" or "control over its economic policy"; and around suspicions about possible connections between the design of the EMU and high levels of unemployment and other economic troubles. The EU's democratic deficit has also been a persistent issue. Control and power seem to have shifted to Brussels and Frankfurt.[9]

It is in the context of continuities and instabilities of public opinion that we should view connections between politico-economic developments, social-psychological mechanisms and cognitive schemes (Figure 2.1). Globalization and neoliberal policies generate uneven growth. Depending on the location, they result in development or underdevelopment and can hasten industrialization or deindustrialization. There is, furthermore, a relatively constant long-term trend of rising productivity. Because of technological developments, more can be produced with fewer workers, and this too can cause deindustrialization. These political economy processes tend to be mutually reinforcing in a range of spatial scales and temporal lengths, often involving unequal and self-reinforcing processes of accumulation of wealth, privileges and power, especially in the absence of countervailing responses. I will discuss the relevant political economy mechanisms in subsequent chapters.

The key problem lies in heightened existential uncertainty and insecurity, which can trigger various social-psychological mechanisms, such as resentment and emotional distancing. These mechanisms transform fear and insecurity and other related negative emotions experienced in specific social circumstances into anger, resentment, and even hatred. Salmela and von Scheve (forthcoming) argue that many fears and insecurities prevalent in contemporary market societies are really about actual or anticipated shame. The affect of shame concerning oneself is repressed and then transformed into generalized resentment and anger against others. This argument must be qualified, however, since fear is similar to shame as an affect that we largely share with other mammals. They are grounded in our neurophysiological structures.

With the capacity to consciously reflect upon the past and future, fear is mixed with the feeling of anxiety and shame with guilt. Shame might have been originally the submissive response to rejection by the hierarchical group. With reflective consciousness and morality, we have the capacity to accumulate memories of being ashamed and anticipate future rejections and their consequences:

> Wrongs, or by another word, sins, or indeed anything that would eject us from society if it were known or seem to eject us from society can be reminisced about out of the past and worried about for the future. And this we call guilt. [. . .] in guilt we can have worry about future shameful experiences, which indeed is anxiety, and we thus have two emotions, anxiety and guilt, coming together as an even more powerful emotion.
>
> (Jaynes 2000, 464–5)

Repressed anxiety, shame and guilt can easily be directed away from the self and toward the other. Anxiety and guilt induce anger and hatred against guilty others and associated groups. In contemporary European and North American contexts these include, in particular, refugees, immigrants, Islamists, greens and leftists, political and cultural elites and the "mainstream" media. This tendency is best seen as an emotional background and context for forming ideas about the causes of anxiety and insecurity. Meaning and self-esteem are sought from aspects of identity perceived to be stable. In the late twentieth and early twenty-first-century contexts, this often means nation or traditional religion. The counterpart is emotional distancing from social identities that are supposed to inflict anxiety and other negative emotions upon one's own self.

Substantial assumptions and related cognitive schemes determine how the causes of insecurity and lack of dignity and recognition are articulated as political claims. Assumptions and cognitive schemes can amount to an ideology that is popular among the wealthy and powerful. An ideology is a system of beliefs and background capacities that misleadingly represents particular aims and interests as universal; it mobilizes structures of meaning to legitimize sectional interests.[10] What is striking is that parallel assumptions and beliefs may also result, under particular circumstances, from the sentiments of anxiety, shame and guilt of the less well-off. This kind of historically contingent convergence of social forces, occurring through the complex, multi-layered and reflexive determinations of public opinion, has involved purposeful and also interest-based attempts to manipulate meanings.[11] This partly explains the shift towards renationalization of politics in the early twenty-first century. Consider the following background assumptions and cognitive schemes that closely connect neoliberalism and populist nationalism:

1. Metaphor: "the nation is a family".[12] This metaphor is arguably key to understanding complex chains of reasoning concerning the value of belonging to the nation, the legitimate role of the government, immigration and many other issues. It is also the basis for such common expressions as "founding fathers", "head of state" and "fatherland" (the term patriot comes from the Latin *pater*, meaning father).
2. Metaphor: "the state is a household".[13] In everyday thinking and in neoclassical economic theory, and particularly in so-called microeconomic theory, states are generally understood as operating within the same constraints as households. It follows for instance that states, like households, are obliged to balance their expenditure to coincide with the income of any given budgetary period.
3. Assumption: scarcity prevails and resources for public purposes such as education and healthcare are fixed and limited.[14] This assumption rationalizes austerity when there is an actual or anticipated public deficit. The same assumption is implicit in claims about migrants taking "our places" in schools or hospitals.
4. Lump of labour fallacy: there is a fixed amount of work to be done within a national economy. This fallacy is presupposed by claims about "they are taking our jobs". (Neoliberals may be less likely to hold this assumption than nationalists).
5. Tendency to blame the weak and vulnerable for economic problems and crises, personification of complex social processes.[15] If markets are free, the world must be just, and thus everyone gets what they deserve. If markets are not free and thus do not function properly, this must be because trade unions suppress free labour markets and government sustains those who do not work. Ordinary workers and dependent people may in turn pass the blame on to migrants and refugees, who are willing to work for less or are, for now, incapable of working.

These assumptions and cognitive schemes make it possible to direct anxiety, shame and guilt away from the self and toward the other. The strict father of the nation[16] must normalize, punish or exclude those who are guilty of straining the resources and inflicting negative emotions upon the blameless members of the community. In the UK popular press, there was little attempt prior to Brexit to differentiate between EU and non-EU immigration. The logic of control of inflows thus could stand in opposition to EU membership, with little knowledge of the actual role of immigration or of the EU required. Deindustrialization also meant that factories relocated to not just China but other parts of Europe. Thus, the EU and technocratic elites in Brussels *must* be responsible for the hardships of ordinary people, even when established elites in London are also criticized.

For causal efficaciousness, it does not matter whether assumptions, metaphors and claims are true or adequate. Moreover, the first-order effects of changing politico-economic circumstances do not have to be particularly widespread to cause a shift in "public opinion". This shift can have self-reinforcing characteristics, yet the emotions spawned by the changing politico-economic circumstances must make sense. The stories told in terms of the basic metaphors and cognitive schemes must appear to explain the vulnerabilities and uncertainties of the situation of those who have been primarily affected. Assuming that global economic liberalism is premised on national powers to limit the movements of people (see Table 2.1), the key contradiction of this belief system lies in assumption 5. It is not only that the free market utopia has played a major role in creating the circumstances that have evoked anxiety, shame and guilt, but also that this utopia makes the poor and vulnerable responsible for their own fate, although they belong to the family-nation – they may be held responsible even when the promises of the market utopia are not realized.

To understand the popularity of parties such as UKIP (see Figure 2.2), it is also necessary to shed light on the dynamics of power relations. Neoliberal

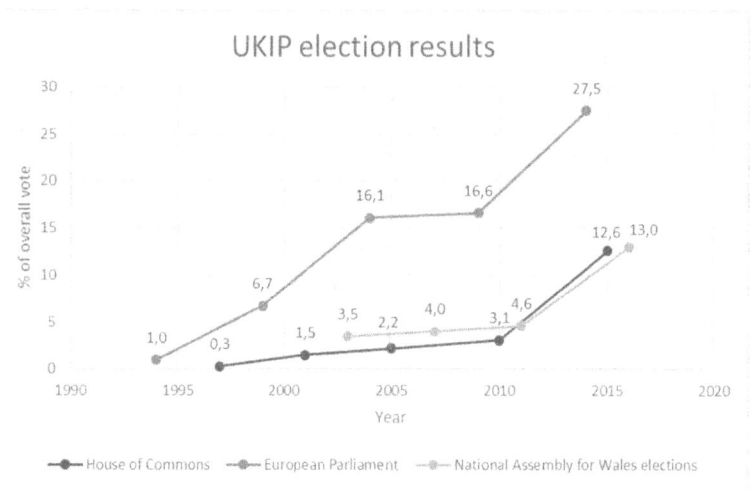

Figure 2.2 The rising popularity of UKIP

globalization is a self-reinforcing process that has changed power relations. The dominant structural position and the direct influence of those who control major businesses has been strengthened. Lobbying has become a £2 billion industry in UK alone (see Sayer 2016, ch 15) The media is increasingly controlled by convergent ideas and interests, as is particularly evident in the case of Rupert Murdoch's media empire (by 2000, Murdoch's News Corporation already owned over 800 companies in more than 50 countries). It is in this context that UKIP arrived on the political scene. Rather than challenging neoliberalism, it has drawn ideas from Thatcher and the right wing of the Conservative Party. UKIP has been built on the assumption that common sense is neoliberal. Private donors such as Paul Sykes, as well as UKIP's early success in the European Parliament elections, helped to secure funding for its activities, thus contributing to UKIP's rise. Commercial and ideological interests may well converge: Murdoch's best-selling daily, the *Sun*, has been a relentless critic of the European Union and all its works. Disputes about the extent of media support to UKIP notwithstanding, important parts of the British media have supported the anti-EU message of UKIP, thus making it credible.

Figure 2.2 depicts the growth of UKIP popularity prior to the referendum. Although UKIP's popularity had already started to rise notably before 2010, the Euro crisis and the turn to austerity in the UK was a turning point (linked also to the decision by the Conservatives to publish a target for annual net migration under Theresa May as Home Secretary of less than 100,000). During the extended crisis that lasted for years it was not difficult to convince people that the EU was a costly project, spelling trouble rather than providing hope. An anti-EU message gained further ground. People voted UKIP despite an electoral system that discourages voting for small parties. Most UKIP-voters knew that their vote would be "wasted". In the 2015 general election, UKIP obtained nearly four million votes (12.6% of the total), replacing the Liberal Democrats as the third most popular party, yet getting only one seat. The 2014 European Parliament elections, despite very low turnout (c. 35%), may better indicate the pre-Brexit popularity of UKIP. In 2014 UKIP secured 27.5% of the votes. The popularity of UKIP and the unpopularity of the EU were strongly correlated, and more than 90% of UKIP supporters voted "leave" in June 2016.

On explaining Brexit in terms of Polanyi's double movement

Ann Pettifor (2017) and other commentators (Colin 2016; O'Reilly 2016; Worth 2017) suggest that Brexit can be understood in Polanyian terms as an attempt of those left behind in Britain to protect themselves from the predatory nature of market fundamentalism. In *The Great Transformation* ([1944] 1957), Polanyi argued that "economic man" and self-adjusting markets are neither natural nor universal. They are relatively recent sociohistorical constructs. The rise of (i) the calculative gain-orientation, (ii) the modern market economy and (iii) the modern liberal state are essentially connected. Prior to the great transformation in modern Europe, markets existed as an auxiliary for the exchange of goods that were otherwise not obtainable. Polanyi claimed that the idea of a self-adjusting market implies a stark utopia annihilating the human, social and natural substance of society. This becomes especially visible during times of great economic change and crises. Society is thus bound to take measures to protect itself against the self-regulating market. Polanyi's double movement consists of the construction of a self-regulating market, followed by a process of social self-protection and decommodification.

Pettifor (2017, 130) argues that "re-regulating the British economy in favour of finance and enriching the 1% while shrinking labour's share of income resulted in rising inequality and lit a still smouldering fuse of popular resentment". Much of her criticism is addressed to neoclassical economists who advocated markets in all spheres of life and economy, including finance. Economist Brad DeLong criticizes Pettifor's position that the Brexit vote was the result of a class- and social structure–based Polanyi process.[17] He uses Germany as an example of a European country that has tacitly but successfully applied a form of Keynesianism. DeLong maintains that there is no economic anxiety in Germany and yet "Angela Merkel is in as much trouble from her indigenous domestic Trumpists as is any centrist political leader in the North Atlantic". On this basis DeLong concludes that the rise of "nativism" (or nationalism) cannot be a Polanyi process.

DeLong's argument is weak. Although Polanyi may have been ambiguous in lumping together all forms of "social protection", nationalism is a chief possibility in his scheme. Moreover, given open systems, politico-economic tendencies necessarily play out in different ways in different contexts. It is true that European industrial activities have been regrouping in and around Germany and that the German unemployment rate is low, but deindustrialization and increasing polarization of household incomes are occurring in Germany too. Some of the income polarization in Germany is directly linked to neoliberal policies such as the deregulation of the labour market, but deindustrialization seems to be one of the drivers of this process. Deindustrialization has weakened Germany's middle-income groups (Gornig and Goebel 2017). Moreover, in Germany atypical employment relations have become increasingly common: short-term contracts, part-time jobs, temporary work, job-creation schemes, mini- and midi-jobs and fictitious self-employment. Much of this amounts to precarization: "Who is not afraid of losing their employment and pension nowadays?" (Müller-Jentsch 2016, 44).

Pettifor's interpretation is nonetheless problematic in one regard: it is not evident that populist–nationalist movements and parties in Europe are trying to protect themselves "from the predatory nature of market fundamentalism". Rather, most of these movements and parties seem to have adopted market fundamentalism as part of their platform. Even though there are left responses – Jeremy Corbyn's and Jean-Luc Mélenchon's rise to frontline mainstream politics, the electoral success of Syriza and Podemos – the UKIP espousal of free markets is typical. This requires explanation. It is not enough to say the main response is misguided.

Briefly, I propose three possible co-explanations. The first concerns a major historical shift of meanings in background discourses. This has occurred via systems of education and media, beginning in the US in the 1960s (George 2013) and spreading to other parts of the world (see Springer, Birch, and MacLeavy 2016). Over time new terms were invented and the neoliberal vocabulary started to dominate public discussions (Eagleton-Pierce 2016). This has transformed common sense, on which populists draw (Hall and O'Shea 2013; Smaldone 2016).

An unprecedented way of seeing society as a market – understood through the categories of neoclassical economics, rational choice theory and business studies – has not only become prevalent but is now largely taken for granted in numerous everyday practices. Seeing society as markets, and government as intrusive, has become dominant for large parts of the population in most countries. Much of neoliberalism treats market rationality as a totalizing principle to be applied to every human activity (see e.g. Amadae 2016). We are all customers now and our voting and marriages are calculative-rational utility-maximizing choices. Being political means trying to get re-elected rather than doing what is right. Calculative gain-orientation seems to be everywhere. The new great transformation remaking market society is spatially more extended and institutionally more entrenched than in the nineteenth century. A new second movement has barely started.

My second explanation of why populist–nationalist movements and parties are so neoliberal stems from the crisis of social democracy. Ever since social-democratic parties started to "modernize" themselves, redefining the movement as a pro-market third way (Moschonas 2002; Ryner 2002), these parties have become less capable of addressing injustice and undemocratic rule, and experienced anxiety, shame and guilt within global neoliberalism.

My third and final explanation concerns available resources. Under prevailing post-democratic circumstances (Crouch 2004), it is easier to gain access to the media and get funding for political activities if one's platform concurs with market thinking. In the 2010s, a number of influential activists and politicians are themselves millionaires or billionaires.

Politico-economic developments in the EU and the role of the Euro crisis

Brexit must be seen in a wider context of politico-economic developments and their consequences in Europe. Forces of disintegration have gained strength not only in the UK but across the EU. Trends, patterns and tendencies are like the UK, although experiences diverge in the details of policies, politico-economic developments and ethico-political responses. The very point of the European integration process has been to channel the multiple and often conflictual European pasts into converging presents. Although the Maastricht Treaty took steps towards building a political community, the Treaty was first and foremost about furthering the freedom and rights of transnational capital and finance. The idea was to create a single market and currency, without any corresponding state structures.

The Maastricht Treaty and its later amendments have turned out to be counterproductive. Subsequent events may have come as a surprise to the designers of the Maastricht Treaty and the EMU, but this course was anticipatable. Many political economists (Cohen 2003, 584–8) warned about inherent problems of the EMU; for example, "the economic impact of the euro [. . .] is likely to be deflationary and destabilising [. . .] and that the social consequences are likely to be deleterious" (Arestis, Brown, and Sawyer 2001, 1). A rough look at economic development in the Eurozone seems to confirm this, as indicated by Table 2.2.

The EMU is a neoliberal experiment in which, for the first time in history, a monetary union has been created without a state or political community. The Eurozone states went from being issuers of currency to mere users of

Table 2.2 The Eurozone output growth and unemployment rate

	Region	1961–1970	1971–1980	1981–1990	1991–2000	2001–2008	2009–2016
Average GDP growth rate at 2010 market prices (%)	EZ-12	5.3	3.4	2.4	2.2	1.8	0.3
	EZ-19					1.8	0.4
Average unemployment rate (%)	EZ-12	2.3	4.0	8.6	9.8	8.3	10.7
	EZ-19					8.5	10.7

Sources: Statistics from European Commission (2017, 14, 28); table adapted from Palley (2017, 3).

a currency and this reduced their economic policy possibilities. The EMU took away the power of its member states to borrow directly from a domestic central bank and to influence interest rates. The EU itself has no right to levy taxes or to decide on fiscal policies. The adoption of Chicago School macroeconomics in the constitutive codes of the European Central Bank has led to an exclusive focus on monetary policy, while limiting its targets and means. The Euro's monetary policy institutions have diminished the space for national fiscal policy and also exposed government finances to market instability. Public spending and deficit use are limited by the Maastricht Treaty. This made the Eurozone an especially vulnerable part of the world economy in the aftermath of the global financial crisis 2008–2009.

Thereafter, the global economic crisis triggered automatic stability mechanisms in EU countries. Moreover, most increased national expenditure to stimulate the economy (but are restricted in how they can do this) generating increased public debt, whilst also providing an asset mechanism for banks and investors. The initial political agenda was dominated by discussions of the need to regulate and tax transnational finance. A second phase of the crisis began in spring 2010, when the credit rating agencies downgraded Greece's credit rating to junk status. Greece was not alone. Ireland, Portugal, Spain and others suddenly faced difficulties in renewing their loans at serviceable interest rates. Austerity followed.

This was the beginning of the long Euro crisis that in dramatic fashion came close to forcing Greece to exit the Euro in summer 2015. The Euro crisis and its unceasing representation in the British media fuelled UKIP-style interpretations of Europe in terminal decline (the past but not Britain's future). Counterfactuals about the June 2016 referendum include: without the Euro crisis and consequent relative loss of faith in the European integration project, a sufficient majority of Britons would have voted "Remain". The apparent paradox of the referendum is that many those who voted "Leave" seem to accept domestic austerity and approve the same market fundamentalist tenets on which the EMU is founded.

Conclusions

It is possible to claim that for historical and identity-political reasons Britain was more liable to exit than most other EU member-states. The UK had a legal option to stay out of the single currency in part precisely because its public opinion has been critical of the EMU. In this chapter I have argued, however, that a historically contingent and possibly temporary convergence of social forces explains the overall shift towards renationalization of politics in the 2010s. Nationalism never disappeared, although its forms have changed. For instance, the neoliberal race to be more "competitive" than other countries is a form of nationalism. Among the wealthy and powerful, especially among those dependent on the City of London, the EU and its proposed regulations and taxes have often been seen to pose a potential hazard, albeit balanced by the City's domination of financial services in Europe.

Many who voted for Brexit are poorly educated or informed and belong to lower or lower-middle income groups. For many, political and economic developments associated with neoliberal globalization have created existential uncertainty and insecurity. Attendant emotions are liable to engender negative othering via powerful social-psychological mechanisms and emotionally and cognitively loaded interpretations. These primary effects do not have to be especially widespread to produce a move toward neo-nationalist populism, which in turn can shape wider public opinion.

Common sense can be incoherent. Incoherence makes common sense, like its more ephemeral counterpart "public opinion", open to educational and other changes in society and, to a certain extent, also open to outright manipulation aimed at manufacturing consent (Herman and Chomsky 1994). Beliefs can contradict practices and vice versa. The master-metaphor of "society is a competitive market" does not ensure coherence. Several of those who hold that unrestrained competition driven by self-interest is the only way to succeed also believe that "we should love our neighbours as ourselves". Some of those who depend on welfare benefits believe that all other claimants are "scroungers" (Hall and O'Shea 2013, 10). Many sufferers of neoliberal globalization routinely assume that in free markets everyone gets what they deserve if "we" can keep the foreigners out. Some anti-elite activists and campaigners seem happy to ally themselves with well-established conservative party libertarianism and global free market and trade policies. Although the nation is metaphorically constituted as a family and economy as a household, the elected government is habitually envisaged as intrusive – at the same time it may also epitomize the strict father who punishes or excludes.

While actors can live with apparent contradictions and paradoxes for extended periods, once recognized, contradictions become a motor for change. Incoherent belief systems are no more stable than political systems lacking principled normative legitimation. For one thing, the more exclusionary and protectionist nationalism becomes, the less consistent it is with free market liberalism. Exclusions and protectionism can also provoke conflicts with different others. Assuming strong resistance or "disorder", conflicts can prompt attempts to regain order forcefully. Struggles over influencing or controlling the media typically become an important aspect of engaging in conflict. Thus contradictions can be temporarily resolved in favour of strict father and family metaphors, meaning that the political system becomes increasingly authoritarian and repressive (cf. Tansel 2017).

National–populist movements or parties may, however, lose part of their purpose, as UKIP did after the 2016 referendum (in combination with the British voting system, this loss of purpose led to UKIP's collapse in the June 2017 general election). National–populist parties may also lose support because the more conventional parties adopt elements of their agenda. They can also lose popular support if their policies appear incoherent, volatile or indistinguishable from mainstream neoliberal policies. Finland is a typical case of the latter. By summer 2017 the support of the Finns Party was halved, following two years in a coalition government with the Centre and Conservative parties, resulting in breakdown of the party in June 2017.

Genuine learning too is possible. Although common sense is deep-seated, it is also contradictory. Public opinion is unstable even when it exhibits continuities. Reality can frustrate ideological fears and hopes. Terrorism may fade away and new jobs emerge in any given time and place. On the other hand, the effects of neoliberal policies, automation and globalization are likely to remain the same despite some degree of national protectionism: restrictions on immigrants, tax reductions, and subsidies for domestically based corporations. These effects can also worsen if a new global economic crisis begins (probable in 2018–2020). Responses through the mechanisms of Figure 2.1 are likely to intensify, and fresh calls for alternatives are also likely to rise. In the process, the dominant background assumptions and common sense are liable to be questioned, and at least some new assumptions and ideas proposed.

Note also that Polanyi (1957, 93) is a reminder that industrialization and the emergence of a truly planetary economy began abruptly in Britain:

> On the eve of the greatest industrial revolution in history, no signs and portents were forthcoming. Capitalism arrived unannounced. No one had forecast the development of a machine industry; it came as a complete surprise. For some time England had been actually expecting a permanent recession of foreign trade when the dam burst, and the old world was swept away in one indomitable surge toward a planetary economy.

Since the second half of the twentieth century, it has been repeatedly realized that an adequate response to the consequences of a planetary economy includes extending the spatial scale of social, ecological and democratic alternatives. Arguably this will be the main theme of twenty-first-century world politics – perhaps in a surprising manner.

Notes

1 The term refers to Joseph P. Overton (1960–2003), a former vice president of the Mackinac Center for Public Policy: a given public opinion makes assumptions about possibilities along an axis unthinkable–radical–acceptable–sensible–popular–policy. During the past decade the concept has been used to purposefully generate a shift toward the libertarian or nationalist right (see Marsh 2016). Cameron's contribution shows that this kind of shift can also happen unintentionally (an attempt to explicitly defeat a rising idea may actually serve to strengthen it).
2 Fiscal policies of the European Central Bank and principles of the EMU are grounded in neoclassical economic theories and rational choice theory. For initial underlying theory see Lucas (1972); Barro (1974); and Sargent and Wallace (1975).
3 Jeremy Corbyn's Labour is ambiguous in terms of the national–cosmopolitan axis. Moreover, the categories of Table 2.1 conceal the possibility of EU-nationalism, which may appear as cosmopolitanism in a traditional national context but could become constitutive of a federal state that involves an emergent hybrid national identity (cf. Britishness vs. Englishness).
4 For UK deindustrialization see Kitson and Michie (2014) and the EEF website factsheet available at www.eef.org.uk/campaigning/campaigns-and-issues/manufacturing-facts-and-figures.
5 The UK has become more unequal than most OECD countries. The peak year of income inequality in the UK was 2001/2. A gradual decline in the Gini coefficient since then has occurred, and perversely via post financial crisis effects; see Office for National Statistics (2017). Note, UK *wealth* inequality has risen continuously (Credit Suisse Research Institute 2016) and income inequality is predicted to rise in the future due to poor wage growth and austerity policies (Jackson 2017).
6 In 2016, the UK GDP per capita was £22746.71, which is near the 2007 level of £22000. Measured in euros, UK GDP per capita was significantly less in 2016 as compared to 2007. See the Trading Economics data at constant UK prices: www.tradingeconomics.com/united-kingdom/gdp-per-capita-at-constant-prices-imf-data.html; Eurostat GDP data € per inhabitant (at market prices, current prices), at http://ec.europa.eu/eurostat/web/national-accounts/statistics-illustrated; and Inman (2017).
7 These developments have been widely reported in the British media, e.g. the *Financial Times* July 2015 "Austerity's £18bn impact on local services. FT analysis reveals local government welfare system creaking under weight of growing demand", available www.ft.com/content/5fcbd0c4-2948-11e5-8db8-c033ed-ba8a6e; and the *Independent* February 2015 "Most deprived English councils suffer biggest cuts in spending power. Knowsley council in Merseyside has seen its income per head fall by more than £400", available at www.independent.co.uk/news/uk/politics/most-deprived-english-councils-suffer-biggest-cuts-in-spending-power-10045665.html.
8 The Genuine Progress Indicator (GPI) is an alternative to GDP (see Kubiszewski et al. 2013). GPI starts with Personal Consumption Expenditures (a major component of GDP) but adjusts them using 24 different components, including income distribution, environmental costs and negative activities like crime and pollution. In many countries, beyond a certain point, GDP growth no longer correlates with increased economic welfare. On a global scale since the late

1970s or 1980s, GPI figures indicate overall regressive rather than progressive developments, in spite of per capita GDP growth. The UK's relatively good GPI performance in 1993–2007 (in sharp contrast to 1976–1992) can be partly explained by positive ecological effects of (i) cleaner technologies and (ii) deindustrialization in the context of (iii) rising personal consumption expenditures (the real effects of this were partly offset by deepening commodification). Note also, during the New Labour years 1998–2010 UK crime rates started to decline, following a period of rapid rise. Moreover, after the peak of 2001/2002 UK income inequalities stopped growing, and declined slowly after 2007. New Labour policies resulted in some social improvements in relation to the previous period.

9 The metaphor "democratic deficit" is deceptive when thinking about future possibilities to democratize the EU. The term "deficit" refers to a quantitative absence, a shortage or gap. It evokes a partially full dish or container. Pour in a bit more, and the deficit is gone. For an alternative framing of the question, and a political economy oriented answer to "can the EU be democratized?", see Patomäki (2014).

10 Apart from misrepresentation of particular interests as universal, also various false beliefs, illusions, mystifications and reifications may be necessary for the reproduction of social practices and institutions that involve asymmetrical resources and domination. False beliefs can evolve, for instance, from the pleading of a pressure group. Illusions of perception, cognitive biases and one-sided substantial beliefs may first become popular within a network or discursive field of positioned actors, can then become part of an *ortodoxa*, finally falling into the common sense and the taken-for-granted background. For a definition of "ideological" in terms of particular/universal interests, see Giddens (1979, 6, 165–97); for a more general definition and discussion of ideology-critique, see Bhaskar (1979, 71–7); for discussion, see Patomäki (2002, ch 6); and for "how we know what isn't so", Gilovich (1991).

11 Human behaviour and thinking can be easily directed through the exploitation and manipulation of framings and metaphors, as advertising and political marketing indicate (Geary 2011, 58–75, 112–36), which is why the control of mass media is a central political question. Moreover, the emergence of internet and social media has opened up new possibilities for subtle and individualized moulding of human thought and action. Cadwalladr (2017) claims that large-scale data mining from Facebook files and other internet-based sources was the basis of targeted political messaging in the "Leave" campaign, securing the tight margin in favour of Brexit. This part of the "Leave" campaign was largely funded by Robert Mercer, a US billionaire and hedge fund owner who was also Donald Trump's biggest donor. Mercer owns a firm called Cambridge Analytica that was central in this operation. Mercer is a friend of Farage and a close associate of Steve Bannon.

12 Lakoff (2002, 153–6, 187–90, 222–5, 272–4).

13 Patomäki (2013, 13–27).

14 Gietel-Bastein (2016).

15 Robinson (1962); the same story and pattern of blame is repeated in international relations, see Chapter 4.

16 According to Lakoff and Johnson (1999, 415 *et passim*), Strict Father family morality has long been dominant in the Western and Christian traditions. Father commands and children must be obedient to Father, but they can also resist,

which necessitates harsh discipline. Strict Father can also serve as a metaphor for morality and/or reason. Thus, for instance, to resist passion, the moral will must be strong; it is the duty of reason to provide discipline.

17 "Grasping reality with both hands," available at www.bradford-delong. com/2016/11/must-read-i-have-concluded-that-i-have-a-strong-disagreement-with-ann-pettifor-here-the-brexit-vote-is-not-the-result-o.html#more (accessed 2 May 2017).

References

Amadae, S. M. 2016. *Prisoner of Reason: Game Theory and Neoliberal Political Economy*. Cambridge: Cambridge University Press.

Arestis, Philip, Andrew Brown, and Malcolm C. Sawyer. 2001. *The Euro: Evolution and Prospects*. Cheltenham: Edward Elgar.

Barro, Robert. 1974. "Are Government Bonds Net Wealth?" *Journal of Political Economy* 82 (6): 1095–117.

Becker, Joachim. 2017. "In the Yugoslav Mirror: The EU Disintegration Crisis." *Globalizations*.

Bhaskar, Roy. 1979. *The Possibility of Naturalism: A Philosophical Critique of Contemporary Human Sciences*. Brighton: Harvester Press.

Cadwalladr, Carole. 2017. "The Great British Brexit Robbery: How Our Democracy Was Hijacked." *The Guardian*, May 7. www.theguardian.com/technology/2017/may/07/the-great-british-brexit-robbery-hijacked-democracy.

Cohen, Benjamin. 2003. "Global Currency Rivalry: Can the Euro Ever Challenge the Dollar?" *Journal of Common Market Studies* 41 (4): 575–95.

Colin, Nicolas. 2016. *Brexit: Doom, or Europe's Polanyi Moment?* The Family Papers No. 022, June 27. https://salon.thefamily.co/brexit-doom-or-europes-polanyi-moment-3e97269e6b67.

Cowley, Jason. 2016. "Michael Sandel: 'The Energy of the Brexiteers and Trump Is Born of the Failure of Elites': The Political Philosopher on Markets, Morality and Globalisation." Interview, *New Statesman*, June 13. www.newstatesman.com/politics/uk/2016/06/michael-sandel-energy-brexiteers-and-trump-born-failure-elites.

Credit Suisse Research Institute. 2016. *Global Wealth Report 2016*. Zurich: Credit Suisse Ag. www.credit-suisse.com/fi/en/about-us/research/research-institute/publications.html.

Crouch, Colin. 2004. *Post-Democracy*. Cambridge: Polity Press.

Eagleton-Pierce, Matthew (2016) *Neoliberalism: The Key Concepts*. London & New York: Routledge.

Eurobarometer. 1996. *Eurobarometer 44*. Brussels: European Commission. http://ec.europa.eu/commfrontoffice/publicopinion/archives/eb/eb44/eb44_en.htm.

European Commission. 2017. "Statistical Annex of European Economy." *Directorate-General for Economic and Financial Affairs*, Spring. https://ec.europa.eu/info/sites/info/files/statistical_annex_ee_spring_2017.pdf.

Gardner, Andrew. 2017. "Brexit, Boundaries and Imperial Identities: A Comparative View." *Journal of Social Archaeology* 17 (1): 3–26.

Geary, James. 2011. *I Is an Other: The Secret Life of Metaphor and How It Shapes How We See the World*. New York: Harper Perennial.

George, David. 2013. *The Rhetoric of the Right: Language Change and the Spread of the Market*. London: Routledge.

Giddens, Anthony. 1979. *Central Problems in Social Theory: Action, Structure and Contradiction in Social Analysis*. Los Angeles: University of California Press.

Gietel-Bastein, Stuart. 2016. "Why Brexit? The Toxic Mix of Immigration and Austerity." *Population and Development Review* 42 (4): 673–80.

Gilovich, Thomas. 1991. *How We Know What Isn't So: The Fallibility of Human Reason in Everyday Life*. New York: Free Press.

Gornig, Martin, and Jan Goebel. 2017. "Deindustrialisation and the Polarisation of Household Incomes: The Example of Urban Agglomerations in Germany." *Urban Studies*, first published online September 20, 2016. doi: 10.1177/0042098016669285.

Hall, Stuart, and Alan O'Shea. 2013. "Common-Sense Neoliberalism: The Battle over Common Sense Is a Central Part of Our Political Life." *Soundings: A Journal of Politics and Culture* (55): 8–24.

Harmes, Adam (2012) "The Rise of Neoliberal Nationalism." *Review of International Political Economy* 19 (1): 59–86.

Herman, Edward S., and Noam Chomsky. 1994. *Manufacturing Consent: The Political Economy of the Mass Media*. London: Vintage Books.

Hix, Simon. 2015. "Britons among Least Knowledgeable about European Union: Would Providing More Information about the EU Make People More Pro-EU, as Many Eurosceptics Fear? The Survey Data Is Unclear." *The Guardian*, November 27. www.theguardian.com/news/datablog/2015/nov/27/brits-least-knowledgeable-european-union-basic-questions.

Inman, Phillip. 2017. "UK Inequality Narrows But Many Working People Are Worse Off: Boost in Pensions Is Main Driver of Rising Standards for Low-Income Groups, ONS Figures Show." *The Guardian*, January 10. www.theguardian.com/uk-news/2017/jan/10/uk-inequality-working-people-pensions-ons#img-1.

Jackson, Gavin. 2017. "How UK Incomes Are Becoming More Unequal: In Six Charts: Pay Squeeze, Tax and Benefit Changes and Housing Costs Will Hit Living Standards." *Financial Times*, February 1. www.ft.com/content/fc4a3980-e86f-11e6-967b-c88452263daf.

Jaynes, Julian. 2000. *The Origin of Consciousness in the Breakdown of the Bicameral Mind*. Boston: Houghton Mifflin.

Kagarlitsky, Boris (2017) Brexit and the Future of the Left, *Globalizations* 14 (1): 110–117.

Kitson, Michael, and Jonathan Michie. 2014. "The Deindustrial Revolution: The Rise and Fall of UK Manufacturing, 1870–2010." Working Paper No. 459, Centre for Business Research, University of Cambridge. www.cbr.cam.ac.uk/fileadmin/user_upload/centre-for-business-research/downloads/working-papers/wp459.pdf.

Kubiszewski, Ida, Robert Costanza, Carol Franco, Philip Lawn, John Talberth, Tim Jackson, and Camille Aylmer. 2013. "Beyond GDP: Measuring and Achieving Global Genuine Progress." *Ecological Economics* 93: 57–68.

Lakoff, George. 2002. *Moral Politics: How Liberals and Conservatives Think*. Chicago: University of Chicago Press.
Lakoff, George, and Mark Johnson. 1999. *Philosophy in the Flesh: The Embodied Mind and Its Challenge to Western Thought*. New York: Basic Books.
Lucas, Robert E. 1972. "Expectations and the Neutrality of Money." *Journal of Economic Theory* 4 (2): 103–24.
Marsh, Laura. 2016. "The Flaws of the Overton Window Theory: How an Obscure Libertarian Idea Became the Go-to Explanation for This Year's Crazy Politics." *New Republic*, October 27. https://newrepublic.com/article/138003/flaws-overton-window-theory.
Mikko Salmela, and Christian von Scheve (forthcoming) "Emotional Roots of Right-Wing Political Populism." *Social Science Information*, in press, available at https://www.academia.edu/31722166/Emotional_roots_of_right-wing_political_populism.
Moschonas, Gerassimos. 2002. *In the Name of Social Democracy: The Great Transformation: 1945 to Present*. Translated by Gregory Elliott. London: Verso.
Müller-Jentsch, Walter. 2016. "Twenty Years of 'Industrielle Beziehungen': Looking Back and Taking Stock." In *Developments in German Industrial Relations*, edited by Ingrid Artus, Martin Behrens, Berndt Keller, Wenzel Matiaske, Werner Nienhüser, Britta Rehder, and Carsten Wirth, 31–68. Newcastle: Cambridge Scholars Publishing.
ONS (Office for National Statistics). 2017. *Statistical Bulletin: Household Disposable Income and Inequality in the UK: Financial Year Ending 2016*. www.ons.gov.uk/peoplepopulationandcommunity/personalandhouseholdfinances/incomeandwealth/bulletins/householddisposableincomeandinequality/financialyearending2016#gradual-decline-in-income-inequality-over-the-last-decade.
O'Reilly, Jacqueline. 2016. "The Fault Lines Unveiled by Brexit." In Discussion Forum: "Brexit: Understanding the Sosio-Economic Origins and Consequences." *Sosio-Economic Review* 14 (4): 808–14.
Palley, Thomas. 2017. "Fixing the Euro's Original Sins: The Monetary-Fiscal Architecture and Monetary Policy Conduct." Working Paper Series No. 431, Political Economy Research Institute, University of Massachusetts Amherst, February. www.peri.umass.edu/publication/item/971-fixing-the-euro-s-original-sins-the-monetary-fiscal-architecture-and-monetary-policy-conduct.
Patomäki, Heikki. 1997. "Emu and the Legitimation Problems of the European Union." In *The Politics of the European Monetary Union*, edited by Petri Minkkinen and Heikki Patomäki, 164–206. Dordrecht: Kluwer.
Patomäki, Heikki. 2002. *After International Relations: Critical Realism and the (Re)construction of World Politics*. London: Routledge.
Patomäki, Heikki. 2008. *The Political Economy of Global Security: War, Future Crises and Changes in Global Governance*. London: Routledge.
Patomäki, Heikki. 2009. "Neoliberalism and the Global Financial Crisis." *New Political Science* 31 (4): 431–42.
Patomäki, Heikki. 2013. *The Great Eurozone Disaster: From Crisis to Global New Deal*. London: Zed Books.

Patomäki, Heikki. 2014. "Can the EU Be Democratised? A Political Economy Analysis." In *The European Union and Supranational Political Economy*, edited by Riccardo Fiorentini and Guido Montani, 116–32. London: Routledge.
Pettifor, Ann. 2017. "Brexit and Its Consequences." *Globalizations* 14 (1): 127–32.
Polanyi, Karl. (1944) 1957. *The Great Transformation: The Political and Economic Origins of Our Time*. Boston: Beacon Press.
Putnam, Robert D. 1988. "Diplomacy and Domestic Politics: The Logic of Two-Level Games." *International Organization* 42 (3): 427–60.
Rasmus, Jack. 2010. *Epic Recession: Prelude to Global Depression*. London: Pluto Press.
Reynolds, David (2017) "Britain, the Two World Wars and the Problem of Narrative." *The Historical Journal* 60 (1): 197–231.
Robinson, Joan. 1962. *Economic Philosophy*. London: The New Thinker's Library.
Ryner, J. Magnus. 2002. *Capitalist Restructuring, Globalization and the Third Way: Lessons from the Swedish Model*. London: Routledge.
Sargent, Thomas J., and Neil Wallace. 1975. "'Rational' Expectations, the Optimal Monetary Instrument and the Optimal Money Supply Rule." *Journal of Political Economy* 83 (2): 231–54.
Sayer, Andrew. 2016. *Why We Can't Afford the Rich*. Bristol: Policy Press.
Sewell, William H., Jr. 1996. "Historical Events as Transformations of Structures: Inventing Revolution at the Bastille." *Theory and Society* 25 (6): 841–81.
Smaldone, Tristan. 2016. "The Occupation of Common Sense: From Neoliberalism to Radical Democracy." *Inquiries Journal* 8 (1). www.inquiriesjournal.com/articles/1329/the-occupation-of-common-sense-from-neoliberalism-to-radical-democracy.
Springer, Simon, Kean Birch, and Julien MacLeavy, eds. 2016. *The Handbook of Neoliberalism*. London: Routledge.
Tansel, Cemal Burak, ed. 2017. *States of Discipline: Authoritarian Neoliberalism and the Contested Reproduction of Capitalist Order*. London: Rowman & Littlefield International.
Thorleifsson, Catherine. 2016. "From Coal to Ukip: The Struggle over Identity in Post-Industrial Doncaster." *History and Anthropology* 27 (5): 555–68.
Watkins, Susan (2016) "Casting off?" *New Left Review* (100): 5–31.
Worth, Owen. 2017. "Reviving Hayek's Dream." *Globalizations* 14 (1): 104–9.

3 EU, Russia and the conflict in Ukraine

The European integration project is not simply reducible to political economy, despite the original EEC focus on trade relations. Functional cooperation has been a means to create a pluralistic European unity to overcome antagonisms that culminated in the catastrophes of World War. But it is through political economy dynamics that this project has become intertwined with specific world-historical developments in the last four decades. The global political economy forms a complex, dynamic process. Actors participate in bringing about and steering global political economy processes. The European integration process is a big part of the world economy; and the EU is an important actor within it.

From the beginning, the EEC (→EC→EU) aimed to contribute to global economic liberalization. This process has been accompanied by enlargement in 1973, 1981, 1986, 1990, 1993, 1995, 2004, 2007 and 2013. As anticipated by Galtung (1973, 8–32), periods of deepening integration and enlargement have followed each other. By the arrival of the Euro, European integration had achieved a single interior market whilst pursuing further trade liberalization beyond EU borders. The Euro crisis and Brexit have disrupted these developments.

The EU can be thought as an actor-in-process that follows its historically evolving inner dispositions and characters. These generate causal processes through which its forms and parts are determined. They also help shape the world economy, in part through unintended consequences of actions, whose feedback affects the EU. Functional cooperation in Europe during the Bretton Woods era was often economistic and premised on liberal economics. However, the period from the breakdown of the Bretton Woods system to the establishment of the Maastricht Treaty was important in re-structuring the inner codes of the EU toward neoliberalism,[1] but also toward European identity and elements of European polity.

The European Neighbourhood Policy (ENP) was preceded by democracy and human rights promotion and "technical" programmes such as TACIS

("Technical Assistance to the Commonwealth of Independent States"). The ENP was conceived in 2004 to manage the continual expansion of the EU. The idea was to foster transition to democratic market-oriented economies. Arguably, the end of this kind of transition is set by standard textbook models of neoclassical economics – in particular perfect competition, which forms the main neoclassical prototype of the economy – and by the parallel normative views of Milton Friedman and Friedrich Hayek.

The goal of transition is also constituted, however, by concepts of democracy, human rights, civil society, good governance, development, sustainability and resilience. Although closely linked to neoliberal discourse (see Eagleton-Pierce 2016; Patomäki 1999a; Patomäki and Pursiainen 1998; Chandler and Reid 2016), these concepts are more open to diverse contestable interpretation than the reductive model of ideal competitive markets. Diversity notwithstanding, a belief in the triumph of the West and liberal End of History (Fukuyama 1989) has tacitly informed transition.

Political and economic ideas and theories have real causal effects through economic policies and regulatory and institutional implications. The literature focussing on the efficiency of EU policies, taking their normative goals as given (e.g. Delcour 2017) recognizes that these policies assume that adoption of EU norms and rules will bring security, stability and prosperity to the EU's Eastern neighbourhood. In this chapter, I argue that the EU's neighbourhood policy and peace strategy is premised on two general hypotheses about the conditions of peace. The first hypothesis states *free trade and free markets foster peace* (the hypothesis of liberal or capitalist peace), and the second *democratic states do not fight each other* (the hypothesis of democratic peace). Both hypotheses are deep-seated. They have guided political activities and sometimes also policies for two centuries. We have ample geo-historical experience in terms of which they can be assessed.

There are reasons to be sceptical about the general validity of these hypotheses, as the case of the conflict in Ukraine illustrates. The Ukrainian conflict has been entangled with NATO and EU expansion eastwards and with Russia and Ukraine's positioning in the world economy. In Russia, the politico-economic disaster resulting from the shock therapy of the 1990s induced a new emphasis on the "strong state", enabling the rise of Vladimir Putin as a "strong leader".

In the early 2000s, post-Soviet Russia still remained committed to closer ties with the neoliberal West and its multilateral organizations. However, the Iraq war of 2003, and the practical exclusion of Russia from Europe as defined by the EU, but expressing NATO and US concerns, led to the disillusionment and alienation of Russia (Sakwa 2016, 30–49). The one-sidedness of EU policies toward its neighbourhood constitutes a form of narrow power, a concept defined by Deutsch (1963, 111):

> Power in this narrow sense is the priority of output over intake, the ability to talk instead of listen. In a sense, it is the ability to afford not to learn.

I begin this chapter by first examining the EU's neighbourhood policy, explicating and assessing the two underlying hypotheses about the liberal conditions of peace. Second, I argue that prevailing ideas and policies have played an unintentional role in aggravating conflict (i) between Russia and the West, including the EU, and (ii) within Ukraine, where these cleavages and conflicts have resulted in actual violence and war. These two conflicts are not separate. They are best seen as processes that are part of the same security complex. It is not even clear who the main parties in Ukraine are.

Third, I explain how prevailing policies have causal effects via the mechanisms of the capitalist market economy. The consequences of the global financial crisis of 2008–2009 and the Euro crisis heightened existential insecurities in and caused an acute financial crisis for Ukraine. These developments provided the politico-economic context for the Euromaidan demonstrations and civil unrest in Ukraine. My point is not to argue for some sort of political economy determinism. Most drastic turndowns or rises in unemployment or precarity do not bring about revolutions or wars, but they do increase the potential for conflict escalation, and this proclivity may actualize if other forces and processes push developments in the same direction.

Fourth, the securitization and geo-politicization of Western policies, and Russia's involvement in the conflict in Eastern Ukraine and its annexation of Crimea, provoked Western sanctions against Russia. These sanctions can be seen as a logical continuation of the conditionality associated with EU's accession and neighbourhood policies. I consider the already materialized and likely future consequences of sanctions. Last but not least, I switch perspective and argue in the conclusion that the absence of adequate global institutions can be a principal cause of what is happening.

EU's neighbourhood policy and the liberal conditions of peace

As an official document, the EU Commission's 2004 European Neighbourhood Policy (ENP) Strategy Paper can be difficult to decode. Such documents are political, reflecting compromises reached in EU institutions, and present EU activity in a positive light in view of likely audiences. Policy documents do not define their central terms; they can make ambiguous claims and contain elements from different, even contradictory, political ideologies. Key terms of the Strategy Paper include security, stability, prosperity and well-being, but their precise meaning can only be inferred from context. The documents contain long lists of values and aims, from liberal trade and good governance to core labour standards and the rights of minorities and children. It is not obvious what the order of importance is.

One way to assess the importance of various aspects and parts of ENP is to look at proposed funding. The Strategy Paper promised to increase project funding channelled through already existing programmes. In 2000–2003 that assistance amounted to about €1 billion a year for 11 countries (EU 2004, 23), roughly 1% of the EU budget, which in turn is about 1% of its GDP. The budget of the City of Helsinki alone is 4–5 times bigger. When the overall sum is divided further between different countries and numerous specific activities, allocation to specific programmes is small, usually meaning minimal impact outside a local context. This suggests that effects through trade, economic policies and rule-harmonization are in general more important than the effects of direct assistance.

When examined in terms of background assumptions and theories, it is often possible to identify clusters of meanings in a political document. Thus the rule of law; a well-functioning and independent judiciary; human rights and fundamental freedoms, including freedom of media and expression; and rights of minorities belong to the standard Western conception of liberal democracy. Although there can be alternative understandings of the rule of law or human rights, or any of the key utterances, it is possible to infer the assumed meaning from context. Moreover, even when a key term such as "good governance" has different possible connotations, one meaning can dominate. Thus "good governance" has meant in effect being governed like the EU and emulating the neoliberalization of existing members.[2]

A political document can involve many ambiguities. The ENP Strategy Paper stresses in several places that "the ENP aims to avoid new dividing lines at the borders of the enlarged Union" (EU 2004, 16). Nevertheless, the starting point of the document is that the external borders of the Union are moving outwards and that Russia and Belarus are being excluded: "We have acquired new neighbours and have come closer to old ones" (EU 2004, 2). Similarly, the document emphasizes that "the EU does not seek to impose priorities or conditions on its partners" (EU 2004, 8), and yet there are explicit conditions. All the values and aims are set by the EU. Convergence means convergence to the prevailing EU model, i.e. convergence with its laws, regulatory structures and underlying ethos. The idea that the "neighbourhood" could change the EU or participate in its decision-making processes is absent. The process is unidirectional (see Cremona and Hillion 2006, 20–3)

The main purpose of the ENP is to promote stability and security. We can infer that this purpose includes peace as the absence of war and violence, even though the term peace is mentioned in the document only once: "The Union's aim is to promote peace" (EU 2004, 12). The EU fosters peace by way of endorsing liberal democracy. Moreover, the ENP also aims to increase prosperity and material well-being, and affluence is associated with peace. The Union sets out to further prosperity and growth by means of free trade, free markets and private-sector led growth. Fighting against corruption, for instance, is represented as a means to increase business confidence.

From this we can conclude that that EU's security and prosperity strategy is premised on two principal hypotheses about the conditions of peace. The first hypothesis states *free trade and free markets foster peace* (the hypothesis of liberal or capitalist peace), and the second that *democratic states do not fight each other* (the hypothesis of democratic peace). These or related hypotheses have been debated in International Political Economy and International Relations since the Age of Enlightenment and Kant. Each hypothesis deserves a brief subsection of its own.

Hypothesis 1: liberal-capitalist peace

Following Napoleon's wars, liberal reformers started to promote free trade as a pacifying force. These and later reformers make two interconnected claims:

(A) free trade benefits everyone except a few with particular special interests within states, and therefore a general harmony of interests prevail; and
(B) free trade and harmony of economic interests are key factors in determining peace and security and thus peace follows from the benefits of free trade.

Claim (A) rests on Ricardian trade theory and its neoclassical extensions, as well as on the generic "efficient market" hypothesis applied to markets in general. David Ricardo (1821) professed the benefits of free trade in terms of comparative advantage. International division of labour can be beneficial to all parties even when there is no absolute advantage, that is, capacity to produce a particular good at a lower absolute cost than another. Free trade is a worldwide universal good.

In the 1930s, Ricardian trade theory was reformulated in terms of marginalist methodology as a general equilibrium mathematical model of international trade (Ohlin [1933] 1952). "New theory of trade" is usually represented as complementary to the Heckscher-Ohlin model and its derivatives. It suggests that governments might have a positive role to play in promoting new industries and supporting the growth of key industries, or in regulating monopolistic practices (Krugman 1979, 1980, 1981). These qualifications notwithstanding, overall "new trade theory" strongly favours free trade (although not necessarily any new free trade agreement). The idea is that free trade enables markets to grow, increases aggregate product diversity, brings benefits from economies of scale and causes real wages to increase.

In the nineteenth century, List ([1841] 1885) founded a counter-tradition by arguing that the "invisible hand" was not generalizable to all nations at the same time, and did not accurately describe actual practices of leading states. List maintained that only political communities of sufficiently large scale can survive and prosper. He stressed that the scale of production and paths of development matter. Private economic interests do not suffice for the gradual, long-term generation of the conditions for successful industrialization, or for constructing a beneficial comparative advantage in the international division of labour. An active protective state is needed. Moreover, economic success is closely related to the military power of a nation. For many, the nineteenth-century rise of the US and Germany provided evidence of this.

Marx argued that inequalities, property, state-formation and organized violence have always been linked: "The existing bourgeois property relations are 'maintained' by the State power, which the bourgeoisie has organized for the protection of its property relations" (Marx [1847] 2008, 80). From Marx's critical political economy viewpoint, international security appears as an outward extension of the same principle. The use of force can create the basis for the expansion of capitalism and world markets. The inner code of the system is expansionary and potentially violent. Imperialism and associated developments that led to the First World War could constitute evidence for this. Whereas for liberals, societal harmony is possible only if private property and fair market competition are ensured by the state, for Marxists, private property is the ultimate reason for state violence. One might also note Polanyi's reading of history ([1944] 2001), according to which a self-adjusting market economy requires that human beings and the natural environment be turned into fictitious commodities – society's attempts to protect itself via the state can also assume militaristic forms and directions.

From the nineteenth-century under-consumption theorists, via Kalecki and Keynes, to contemporary post-Keynesians and other heterodox economists, the central point is that underutilization of capacity is the norm in the capitalist market economy (Khan and Patomäki 2010). In modern, complex and interdependent systems where the whole is more than the sum of its parts, this kind of underutilization results from the overall lack of effective demand for goods and services. The EU economy during recent decades seems to support this.

It is always possible for states to try to export their economic problems to other states, or even expand their sources and markets by violent or imperial means, but attempts to do so tend to result in a fallacy of composition, often resulting in conflicts among states and other actors (Markwell 2006). Uncertainty about the future, inequalities and endogenous money play an active role in open systems in which strict predictions are not possible, but some characteristic effects can nonetheless be (reflexively) anticipated. These include boom-and-bust cycles in finance (Kindleberger 2000; Minsky 2008). In any case, claim (A) is contestable.

Regarding claim (B), empirical studies have found some evidence for the liberal free trade thesis, yet overall the search for invariant connections (or simple and stable correlations, often amounting to reduction to monocausal explanations) has been unsuccessful – even when the assessment is conducted within standard neoclassical or related conceptual frameworks. Further distinctions and auxiliary hypotheses must be made to account for the lack of simple non-changing regularities. For instance, Gerald Schneider (2014) distinguishes between different cases of the freedom of commerce, internally and externally. Internally the distribution of income, and externally the nature of the traded goods, are among the factors that tend to shape the outcome. Moreover, in debates about the merits of the thesis of what is often called "capitalist peace", many liberal scholars argue that ultimately what matters most for peace, on the basis of evidence, is democracy rather than trade (Dafoe, Oneal, and Russett 2013; Ray 2013).

The crux of the matter is that, in the absence of closed systems in society, decisive tests between theories are hard to come by. This enables ideological positions to evolve easily and fortify themselves rapidly. Assessments and critical discussions about hypotheses become complex, interweaving philosophical assumptions, conceptual-theoretical frames, normative aspirations, historical understandings and empirical studies of varying degrees of generality (see Patomäki 2016a). Empirical studies are more typically retrodictive (past-oriented and explanatory) rather than predictive. It is the task of the investigator to explicate interconnections and joint outcomes of a number of historically evolving practices, institutions and structures that are usually already known to exist, and that are causally efficacious in systems that are open to varying degrees, in which simple procedures to test hypotheses or their underlying theories are absent (Arestis, Brown, and Sawyer 2002).

Criticism by empirical means is possible, but difficult; and "empirical" also concerns interpretations of macro-historical evidence. For instance, some economic crises may have dramatic political consequences, such as those that followed the Great Depression and contributed to the coming of World War II (Moser 2016).

Hypothesis 2: democratic peace

Many liberal scholars argue, on the basis of historical evidence, that what matters is democracy rather than trade (Patomäki 2016b). Democratic peace theory experienced a renaissance after the end of the Cold War and collapse of the Soviet Union. Doyle (1983a, 1983b, 1986) became famous for restating the argument that liberal democratic states are different. "They are indeed peaceful" (1986, 1151), even if only in relations amongst themselves. Liberal states have been involved in numerous wars with non-liberal states; and liberalism may constitute a form of patriotism and crusading spirit against different others, generating violent conflicts. But if world history is moving in a liberal democratic direction, and if wars among liberal states are highly unlikely, there is hope for perpetual peace.

Doyle's definition of a liberal democratic state was broad, including social democracy and democratic socialism. However, often the understanding of democracy is narrower, if not ethnocentric, along the lines of "the United States is the premier democratic country of the modern world" (Huntington 1991, 29–30). The democratic peace hypothesis and various supporting theoretical understandings have been debated over the last 25 years. The majority of IR and peace researchers agree that an empirical connection roughly holds within a specified time–space frame (two limited waves of democratization since the late eighteenth century and a globally more widespread third wave since the 1980s) despite that no sufficient or necessary condition for the absence of war has pertained. The most important exception to the empirical rule are the many cases of US quasi-imperialist interventions – or covert measures – against democratic and popular regimes in the global south (Rosato 2003, 590–1; Doyle 2005, 465).

Barkawi and Laffey (1999) argue that states participating in the "peace zone" have evolved as part of globalizing social processes that are constitutive of their inner structures, while also connecting their development and powers to the dynamics of the world economy and its governance. In this globalizing process, state capabilities, including their coercive powers, may come to be reorganized internationally, transnationally or supranationally. What is more, the transformed states may be – or may come to be seen as – less democratic than before, and thus become more easily redefined as enemies.

The idea of a liberal democratic zone of peace has been replicated in the ENP:

> EU's task is to make a particular contribution to stability and good governance in our immediate neighbourhood [and] to promote a ring of well governed countries to the East of the European Union and on the borders of the Mediterranean with whom we can enjoy close and cooperative relations.
>
> (EU Commission 2004, 6)

Developments in countries such as Ukraine, Russia, Egypt and Libya (or Iraq and Syria) have not followed the envisaged path. The relevant globalizing processes, democracy and the political economy conditions for war and peace are interwoven in complex ways. While there may be no simple underlying political economy cause determining the democracy–peace nexus, we know that economic practices and the positioning of states in the changing division of labour in the world economy condition possibilities for democracy, thus affecting peace (see Mousseau 2003; Mousseau, Hegre, and Oneal 2003; Lees 2013). These arguments leave ample room for other causes of democracy and democratic values. They can also be made compatible with the long-term trend of the declining importance of war and violence in human society (Pinker 2011). What they imply, however, is that democracy in a globalized world cannot be thought of in isolationist or stationary terms. The world is an open dynamic process within which its active and responsive parts, such as states, are enfolded. An implication is that political economy and our beliefs about it matter and the latter is not reducible to the former.

The political economy dynamics of Russia vs the West

To understand the conflict in Ukraine, we need to go back in time to the early 1990s. In Russia as well as in Ukraine, the initial private wealth distribution that resulted from "shock therapy" and the privatization of state assets caused turmoil and counter-reactions. When the authoritarian and repressive Soviet system collapsed, the transformation was influenced by the neoliberalizing West and authorized by Boris Yeltsin and associated economic liberals (Leonid Kravchuk played this role in Ukraine). Trade was opened and state price and currency controls were replaced by private property and self-regulating markets. Capital was concentrated in the hands of those few who could command resources to buy ownership-shares, typically either nomenklatura members and insiders, or former black market racketeers. Privatization and "shock therapy" resulted in rapid deindustrialization and a 40% decline in GDP; a vast jump in inequality and spread of mass poverty; and hyperinflation. For years property rights remained vague and contested. Those who came to be called "oligarchs" repeatedly found themselves in a state of war against other oligarchs, literally arming themselves against their rivals.[3]

It is plausible to claim that in established capitalist market societies inequalities of income and wealth among individuals and social classes tend to accumulate, although this is no iron law, but a mere open-systemic tendency. Thomas Piketty (2014) claims that there is a tendency for $r > g$, where r is the average annual rate of return on capital and g is annual economic growth (for a discussion on Piketty's claim, see Chapter 5). In a typical historical process, past wealth seems to become increasingly important and inherited wealth grows faster than output and income. If this is combined with the inequality of returns on capital as a function of initial wealth, the result is an increasing concentration of capital. Mathematically and overly simplistically, this is simply a product of compounding; realistically, it is a complex conditional process of power likely to lead to the accumulation of political privileges and hence de-democratization. The trend towards increasing inequality is difficult to reverse.

In most OECD countries inequalities have been rising since 1980 (most notably in 1980–2000), although not always in a linear manner. In Russia after the abrupt and dramatic rise of inequalities in wealth and incomes in the early 1990s, income inequalities declined somewhat in the late 1990s, partly because of the 1998 financial crisis. Following Putin's rise the socio-economic situation initially stabilized. This stabilization was widely supported by experts and citizens alike, and accompanied by a restoration of some state controls in the economy; simultaneously Putin's regime made entrepreneurial activity easier. Devaluation and the rise of the price of oil and other commodities in world markets then enabled growth, and this had knock on effects for ordinary citizens. In the 2010s, the income distribution of Russia is similar to the US. In Ukraine, the Gini index has been, and remains, much lower, but the concentration of wealth has become even more skewed than in Russia.[4]

The changes from 1995 to the early 2000s involved an ideological rethink in Russia. Yeltsin concluded as early as 1997 that "in order to make the transition to stable economic growth, economic freedom alone is insufficient. We need a new economic order. And for this, strong and intelligent power is needed and a strong state." The modernizers (*zapadniks*) of the 1990s started to advocate state authoritarianism.[5] During Yeltsin's era in the 1990s, however, relations among oligarchs and various factions within Russia continued to be intensely antagonistic. The party that assumed control after Yeltsin was named "United Russia" (at first simply "Unity", its main competitor then being "Fatherland – All Russia"). For nearly two decades, Putin has been its figurehead, although other politicians such as Sergey Shoygu, Boris Gryzlov and Dmitry Medvedev have also chaired the party. The consolidation of Putin's power in the early years involved a "grand bargain" with then powerful oligarchs combined with state sanction for those whose wealth and influence challenged the Kremlin.

Shifts in relations of power shape the selection of dominant beliefs, narratives and discourses. Nationalism warrants unity and a strong state. The subsequent move towards nationalism in Russia has been articulated within the existing liberal constitution of 1993 and, internationally, in terms of great power pluralism and power-balancing. Many liberals were disappointed with Western policies toward Russia and especially with NATO enlargement.[6] More and more often universalizing Western liberalism came to be perceived as one-sided and skewed toward particular interests and values. The various disillusionments of the first half of the 2000s turned Russia into what Sakwa (2016, 30–4) calls a "neo-revisionist" state, criticizing the one-sided application of rules of the international system rather than trying to drastically change those rules.

United Russia reconsidered Western models of democracy and free markets based on the specific circumstances, problems and aspirations of Russia. These reconsiderations included a Listian concern with Russia's place in the international division of labour: a strong state is required to benefit from Russia's natural resources; to further develop space and military technologies; and to diversify the industrial base.[7] United Russia has maintained that Western liberal universalism is wrong. The world is characterized by a plurality of different values. Russia's role in the world is to preserve value pluralism and protect the interests of the Slavic-Orthodox world – by force, if there is no better alternative (see e.g. Kuchins and Zevelev 2012).

After Yeltsin, Russian leadership has been progressively determined to undercut NATO and limit EU expansion.[8] This is connected to an interpretation of political changes not only in the former Soviet Union but also in the Balkans during the early 2000s. The Kosovan war in 1998–1999 – occurring in the aftermath of the Asian financial crisis of 1997–1998 that hit Russia hard – constituted a turning point in Russian politics. Since the early 2000s, Russian state leaders have been predisposed to interpret the so-called colour revolutions in Serbia, Georgia, Ukraine and elsewhere as a deliberate strategic European eastward expansion. In the words of Foreign Minister Sergei Lavrov: "The US and Europe use the 'Color Revolution' to serve their own interests, impose their own values, and end in creating new global tensions" (Cordesman 2014).

Some involvement is evident, but the precise extent to which uprisings in the early 2000s in Serbia, Georgia, Ukraine and elsewhere were in fact supported, encouraged, funded or even systematically planned by the US and the EU or its member states remains disputed. What we know for sure is that the securitization of these uprisings on the Russian side have triggered exceptional countermeasures,[9] which in turn have led to unintended counterproductive effects, not least in Georgia and Ukraine (Delcour and Wolczuk 2015). The universalizing inner grammar of Western neoliberalism – manifest in various free market arrangements, neighbourhood policies and programmes of democracy and human rights promotion – has become contested and geo-politicized. In its neo-revisionism Russia nonetheless continues to combine elements of state capitalism and neoliberalism in its economic policies and institutional arrangements.

It is evident that many corporate and state actors benefit (or would benefit) from easy or privileged access to raw materials, cheap labour, industrial capacity or markets in Central Eastern Europe, the former Soviet Union and the Balkans. Constructivists are right in stressing that interests are not separate from beliefs but constituted by them (Wendt 1999, 119–38). Interest-constituting beliefs are often disputed. For instance, EU's democracy-promotion is built on the neoliberal model of market society. It allows for some pluralism and exploration of extra-liberal ideas, and this is what civil society actors often do. And yet, there are reasons why "all such ideas are swiftly returned to the magnetic field of (embedded neo)liberal core assumptions" (Kurki 2012, 172). Particular beliefs may come to be selected and pushed because they accord with powerful already-constituted interests. Political economy explanations should not be reductionistic. They must take the concept-dependency of social beings seriously. Explicit interests are mere moments in on-going social processes; and yet interests do have causal-explanatory power.

The political economy dynamics of the Ukrainian conflict and war

The Ukrainian conflict has been entangled with NATO and EU expansion eastwards and with Russia's and Ukraine's positioning in the world economy. The economy of the Eastern part of Ukraine is entangled with Russia, whereas the Western part is geared towards the EU. Large-scale violence in Ukraine began 2014, preceded by student beatings late 2013. More generally, violence was preceded by the "colour revolution" 2004–2005 and the global financial crisis 2008–2009. Financialization deepened and has progressively synchronized boom-and-bust cycles. Figure 3.1 shows Ukrainian GDP collapsed by almost 15% in 2009, ending a decade of economic growth and poverty-reduction.

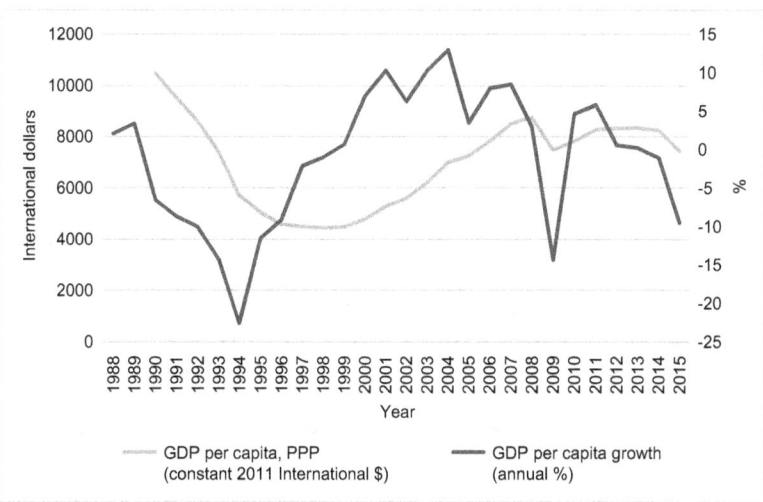

Figure 3.1 Ukraine's GDP per capita and growth rate
Source: Data from World Bank 2017, *World Development Indicators*, at http://databank.worldbank.org/data/

The financial crisis was a decisive turning point in Ukraine's economic development. Rapidly falling prices for Ukraine's major export, steel, led to a substantial deterioration in Ukraine's current account. By late autumn 2008 Ukraine's banking sector verged on collapse. The IMF's fast-track Emergency Financing Mechanism approved a 16.4 USD billion loan in November 2008. The conditions for this loan included a target balanced budget in 2009, to be achieved by expenditure restraint and a phased increase in energy tariffs.

This had a strong regressive impact on income distribution. The loan was frozen after a year because of IMF dissatisfaction. Further loan packages were approved, August 2010 (15.1 USD billion, but again payments were stopped after a year), and, following the acute crisis of late 2013, April 2014 (17.1 USD billion). By 2013–2014 the IMF and the EU were demanding strict austerity and extensive neoliberal reforms: abolition of subsidies, deregulation and privatization, but also measures against widespread corruption. The Association Agreement and related aid and loan packages were tied to IMF conditions.

A recent study (Bogdan and Landesmann 2017) estimates that the radical fiscal adjustment of 2014–2015 has diminished Ukrainian GDP by roughly

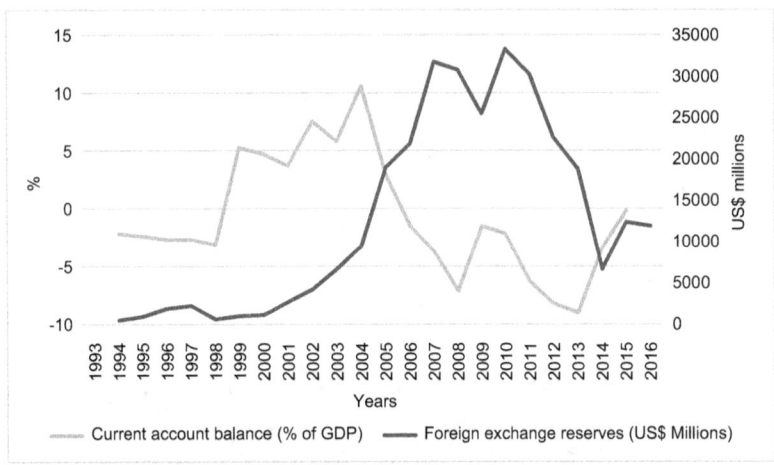

Figure 3.2 Ukraine's current account balance and foreign reserves
Sources: Data for Current Account Balance from World Bank http://data.worldbank.org/indicator/BN.CAB.XOKA.GD.ZS?locations=UA; Data for Foreign Exchange Reserves from IMF http://data.imf.org/regular.aspx?key=60998114.

10%. The earlier IMF loan arrangements likely had similar, albeit smaller effects on GDP. Following a short-lived, partial recovery in 2010–2011, the economic downturn continued parallel with, and was partly caused by, the Euro crisis. Ukraine faced a situation of mounting debt and rapid loss of currency reserves (see Figure 3.2).

Current account in Ukraine reached a record low of -6 USD billion in the third quarter of 2013. At the same time, foreign currency reserves were rapidly approaching a twenty-year record low of 5 USD billion. A debt crisis in a sovereign state such as Ukraine easily becomes self-perpetuating: more loans are given just to service and pay back the previous ones. At the same time, the conditions of those loans mean GDP decline, falling state revenues and increasing expenditures. Everyday life is affected by high levels of unemployment and uncertainty. This kind of downward spiral can last for years (see Patomäki 2013, 133–63).

As Figure 3.1 indicates, 2000–2008 the Ukrainian economy grew 4–10% per year, with industrial production growing over 10% annually. The Davies hypothesis states revolutions are most likely to occur when periods of improvements concerning economic and social development are supplanted by a period of sharp reversal. With the sudden and sharp reversal, a gap between growing needs and actual reality emerges. People exhibit "a mental state of anxiety and frustration when manifest reality breaks away from anticipated reality" (Davies 1962, 6), forming the basis of revolutionary unrest. Developments in Ukraine seem to fit this pattern. Demonstrations started after the Ukrainian government suspended preparations for signing of the EU Association Agreement on 21 November 2013. Following a few years of decline and uncertainty, the acute phase of the fiscal crisis coincided with the Euromaidan demonstrations.

Davies seems to have assumed that people are mostly concerned with maximal needs-satisfaction,[10] but unemployment and economic uncertainties also generate negative social and emotional effects – anxiety etc. Unemployment is an issue of existential security and thus creates room for resentment, emotional distancing and securitization of political issues.[11] In the Ukrainian context, economic hardship is also easy to associate with corruption and concentration of wealth, and thus with a strong anti-elite sentiment. This sentiment aligns with the typical populist split of "people vs. elites", but in Ukraine the elite is divided – usually in accordance with wider societal cleavages.

In functionally differentiated capitalist market societies, economic problems can become threatening to identity. Not only one's earnings but also social worth, rights and duties are tied to a position as an employee, entrepreneur or capitalist. Economic troubles can endanger social integration also because many integrative functions are secured by market-based or tax-revenue dependent public organizations (Habermas 1988, 20–31). Problems of social integration and especially a threatened identity translates easily into existential insecurity, providing fertile ground for processes such as securitization of social issues or Manichaean narratives.[12] Actors can bring about securitization by presenting something as an existential threat and by dramatizing an issue as having absolute or very strong priority. Securitization is always about identity politics; it reinforces a "we".

These considerations give credence to a two-phase causal mechanism hypothesis, selectively efficacious in contemporary open geo-historical contexts. Human actors are reflexive, so circumstances can be variously experienced and interpreted. The two phases of the mechanism described in Figure 3.3 are connected causally, but at the level of meanings, they can be largely disconnected.[13] The category "economic trouble and crisis" involves both subjective experience (trouble) and objective effects (downturn and crisis). Unemployment, fear of unemployment, employment precarity and increasing inequalities perceived as "falling behind" can spell trouble from the viewpoint of those experiencing the hardship.

Social class positioning matters morally (Sayer 2009). It also predisposes actors to forms of learning and breeds characteristic forms of trust or distrust towards established institutions. Pathologies of socialization and existential

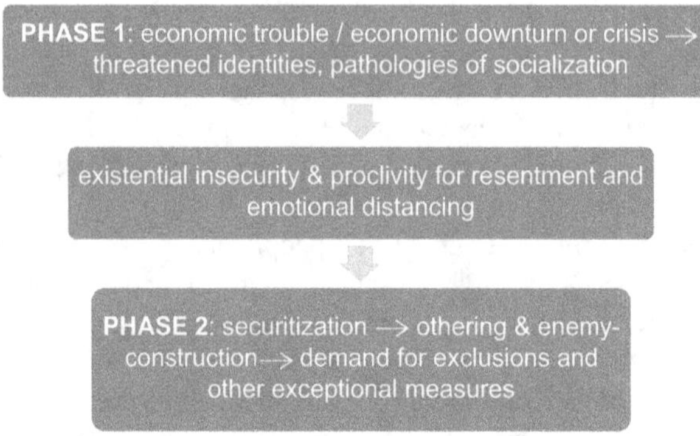

```
┌─────────────────────────────────────────────────┐
│ PHASE 1: economic trouble / economic downturn or crisis → │
│ threatened identities, pathologies of socialization       │
└─────────────────────────────────────────────────┘
                          ⇓
        ┌───────────────────────────────────────┐
        │ existential insecurity & proclivity for resentment and │
        │ emotional distancing                  │
        └───────────────────────────────────────┘
                          ⇓
            ┌───────────────────────────────────────┐
            │ PHASE 2: securitization → othering & enemy- │
            │ construction → demand for exclusions and    │
            │ other exceptional measures                   │
            └───────────────────────────────────────┘
```

Figure 3.3 A two-phase causal mechanism leading to securitization and other-blaming

insecurity can expose "ego" to securitization and to stories that are composed either from older national layers of meaning or from transnationally circulating new stories (such as the threat of political Islam), apparently "explaining" the experiences of vulnerability and insecurity. Commercial and social media play a key role in the dispersion of these kinds of ideas, especially to the extent that they can sustain positive feedback loops (attention drawing attention) and thus generate self-reinforcing processes. Violence dramatically exposed in the media can further inflame the process of othering. To share related sentiments of "us" vs. "them" can also be cherished as democratic; as being on the side of the "people". A further problem is that within context, there may be many "peoples", conceived in terms of ethnic belonging or nations.

The Euromaidan protests started November 2013, when Ukrainian president Yanukovych began to reconsider a negotiated EU association agreement, opting for closer Russian ties. The EU had offered a relatively small loan, with conditions like those imposed by the Troika on Euro crisis countries.[14] Criticism of those conditions fed into East–West and other divides in Ukrainian political economy and society. In February 2014, Ukraine appeared increasingly on the brink of civil war.[15] Violent clashes between protesters and special police forces led to deaths and injuries. Yanukovych fled to Russia, or was ousted, a matter of interpretation, given he was removed from office by parliament, and this probably violated the then constitution. An Association Agreement was then signed with the EU, with extensive political, economic and legal content. The Agreement included a Deep and Comprehensive Free Trade Area (DCFTA).

In March 2014, in response to the removal of Yanukovych, the Supreme Council of Crimea organized a referendum. Thirteen members of the United

Nations Security Council voted in favour of a resolution declaring the referendum invalid, but Russia vetoed it and China abstained. A majority in Crimea seem to have favoured joining Russia, although figures are contested. Probably a clear majority of those who voted supported a Russian Crimea, but if the turnout was as low as 30–50%, only a minority explicitly agreed.[16] Russia hastily made Crimea a part of the Russian federation, irrespective of international law, arguing that the unilateral Kosovo declaration of independence in 2008 set a precedent.

Concurrently, pro-Russian movements, involving Russian citizens, were protesting against Kiev in the Eastern and Southern parts of Ukraine. The precise roles of popular movements, provoked by Kiev's anti-Russian language policies and neoliberal economic policies, and Russia itself, remain disputed. In the East, the situation soon escalated into an armed conflict between separatist militia supported by Russia, at times led by Russians, and the new Ukrainian government. The war in Donbass started in April 2014, continuing as a low intensity conflict in 2017.

EU's role in destabilizing Russia–West relations and Ukraine

The EU, and the West more generally, has taken for granted the universal validity of liberal ideas about free markets and democracy in their policies vis-à-vis Russia, the CIS countries and Eastern Europe. The EU has been externalizing its inner dispositions, which has constituted the essence of its expansion and neighbourhood policy. Seen as a peace project, it consists of two related parts: liberal-capitalist peace and liberal-democratic peace.

Hence, the EU has been trying to impose specific interests and normative purpose as universal and global (cf. Ashley 1989). The conflict between Russia and the West is a result of an interplay between constitutive and causal effects of this purpose, which can also be understood as defining a world order model (cf. Biersteker 2014). At the end of the Cold War and at the time of the collapse of the Soviet Union, this normative purpose was briefly widely accepted in Russia. The politico-economic effects and failure of "shock therapy" led to reassessments and revisions, as did the tendency of the US and EU members to use military force to impose their preferred world order model, often in apparent contravention of international law. Subsequently the Putin regime has resorted to a pluralism articulated in terms of theories and practices of power-balancing, emphasizing the importance of regions and their special characteristics. With the on-going expansion of the EU and NATO towards Russia, Russia has become concerned to draw a line.

Moreover, the Russian government has tended to see "colour revolutions" as a key means of US-led Western expansion involving the EU, and has thus securitized the internal developments of countries such as Ukraine. The universalizing neoliberal orientation of the EU's external relations and expansion has come to be contested and geo-politicized. The EU in turn, and the West more generally, finds Russia's line unacceptable, because it seems to imply a return to nineteenth/early twentieth-century–style power politics. Sakwa responds to this allegation on behalf of Russia by making a distinction between the US-led project of liberal globalization and the security order centred on the US:

> The genius of this US global dualism is that it can pursue traditional geopolitical goals of great-power maximisation (the nineteenth century model) while claiming to be serving the dispassionate interests of the liberal-internationalist order (the claimed post-Westphalian, twenty-first century globalised system).
>
> (Sakwa 2016, 216)

This dualism applies also to the EU. The EU neighbourhood policy involves securitization and explicit discussion of expanded borders. Already in 2004, this policy was conceptually tied to the Common Foreign and Security Policy. While many security threats are represented as common with Russia and other countries, such as "terrorism and its root causes, proliferation of weapons of mass destruction and illegal arms exports" (EU Commission 2004, 13), there is a border between inside/outside. Risks and threats are represented as coming from the outside. A more recent strategy paper acknowledges that "the idea that Europe is an exclusively 'civilian power' does not do justice to an evolving reality" (EU 2016, 2). Actors representing the EU may continue to associate the EU with a post-Westphalian, non-territorial, twenty-first-century globalized system, but the effects of their own acts of border-drawing and securitization are not under their control; meanings and dispositions have real causal (unintended) effects.

Effects tend to reinforce each other; they involve positive feedback loops and cumulative causation. The global financial crisis of 2008–2009 resulted from a self-reinforcing process; it and the Euro crisis and their local consequences inflamed conflicts within Ukraine in a context where outside forces were actively involved. This made the international clash of geo-political visions about the role and place of Ukraine acute.

Effects of sanctions on Russia

Following the annexation of Crimea in March 2014 and the beginning of the war in Eastern Ukraine, the West has imposed rounds of sanctions upon Russia, to which Russia has tried to respond in kind. Research on the real effects of economic sanctions has been published in the International Relations field. One general conclusion is that if the goal is to bring about a desired policy change, the effects of sanctions are complex, unpredictable and often counterproductive (Jones 2015). Even optimists who believe that "our understanding of economic sanctions has progressed significantly over the past three decades" (Morgan 2015, 744) admit the manifold conditions and contributing factors that successful sanctions have. It may thus be contended, typically, that costly, multilateral and effective embargoes against small developing countries work better than other sanctions, but there are many well-known counter-examples from Cuba to Myanmar.

Sanctions can impoverish countries (Gordon 2016), increase inequality (Afesorgbor and Mahadevan 2016) and kill people in need of adequate care and medication (Shahabi et al. 2015). Sanctions can constitute a form of violence (cf. Galtung 1969). They may contribute to (possibly democratic) regime and leadership change (von Soest and Wahman 2015), but most research concludes they are either ineffective or have negative impact on the level of democracy in targeted authoritarian countries (e.g. Peksen and Drury 2010). This should come as no surprise if it is acknowledged that sanctions often result in rallying around the flag (cf. Mueller 1970), whilst also triggering repression. We also know that economic troubles can further securitization and enemy-construction and contribute to conflict escalation. Moreover, the more comprehensive the sanctions, the greater the incentive to violate them.

These and other criticisms have led to the more restrictive idea of "targeted sanctions", which is also the principal approach against Russia. The idea is to directly impact elite interests and specific individuals: financial sanctions, travel bans, restrictions on luxury goods imports, arms embargoes, specific targeting of individuals, corporations or holding companies associated with government leaders etc. In an interdependent world, even targeted sanctions can still have extensive humanitarian consequences (Drezner 2015).

Where sanctions seem to work, effects remain relatively difficult to disentangle from other developments. Recently, Iran concluded an agreement on its nuclear facilities with the West. It appears that sanctions did play a role; but other causes apply, such as developments in Iranian domestic politics and economy and *altercasting* (shaping the Other's perception of one's own identity and interests), so sanctions may be a contributing but not sufficient cause of some achieved goal. Compromise and responsiveness from both parties were then required (Hafner 2015).

What, then, is the likely impact of Western sanctions on Russia? So far sanctions have exacerbated the effects of low oil prices and other economic difficulties. Growth declined to 0.7% in 2014 and -3.7% in 2015, but reversing thereafter.[17] In contrast to authoritarian stereotypes, Putin and other

Russian leaders have won multiparty elections and remain popular. Bloomberg reported May 2016 that Putin's approval rating was "down" to 80%.[18] However, noting a rally-around-the-flag effect, Putin's approval rating was 86.1% in the last week of February 2017.[19]

In response to sanctions, Russia has sought to strengthen relations in Asia. "In experiencing Western hostility but Eastern friendliness, Russia mitigates the damage caused by the sanctions" (Wang 2015, 1). The EU has been Russia's biggest trading partner, since the imposition of the sanctions trade with China has risen but fallen with the EU. The EU accounted for 52.3% of all foreign Russian trade in 2008, falling to 44.8% in 2015 (impacting some EU members more than others: Finnish goods exports to Russia nearly halved 2012–2016, but trade between the two countries then started to rapidly recover).

Most Russians oppose sanctions as hostile, and Russia has been gradually disintegrating from European interactions and processes, becoming more dependent on Chinese and Asian developments. Since no-one seems to be expecting a return of the Crimean to Ukraine, Western sanctions seem first and foremost a factor in a mutual process of conflict escalation. It is no longer exceptional to anticipate war with Russia (e.g. Shirreff 2016), major asymmetries notwithstanding. The combined population of the US and pre-Brexit EU population is six times that of Russia, and spends roughly ten times more on the military.

Given the evidence, are sanctions against Russia justified, in spite of obvious risks and costs? The strongest reasonable argument for sanctions is in fact quite weak: something had to be done because Russia violated international law. This argument implies that it is wrong for any country to destabilize another and intervene militarily (without UN authorization), a position that is only credible if it applies with equal force to the US, to the EU and its members. We also know that sanctions don't usually work in any simplistic isolated sense. Justification, moreover, must also consider what it would be appropriate to do rather than just whether what was done was appropriate.

Conclusions: the role of the absence of adequate global institutions

The EU continues to promote particular contestable ideas as universally valid, even though these have attenuated growth and spawned disintegrative tendencies within the EU. Russia, opposed to universal liberal claims and related double standards and forms of self-righteousness, advocates pluralism via classical–realist multipolarity and power-balancing. Competing world order models involve interpretative principles and purposes that can be incompatible. Moreover, a world order generates real-world socioeconomic effects. The neoliberal governance of the world economy is shaping processes of growth, generating imbalances and uneven developments, and amplifying oscillations in economic activity. The problem is twofold: (i) how do we avoid false universalisms and pluralize context-specific attempts at universalization? and (ii) how should we govern the world economy in order to alleviate, counter or avoid various conflict-generating economic developments?

The golden rule of diplomacy is that one should always grasp how things look from the point of view of others (Morgenthau 1948, 440). What is lost when double standards are practiced or used as a pretext, and when enemies are socially constructed, is the ethico-political ability to see things from others' perspective.

One lesson seems clear: the EU should cultivate its capacity to recognize and accept ethical, political and economic differences, including those concerning the conditions of socio-economic development and progress. Given the constitutive relationship between EU's internal economic policies and its economic neighbourhood policies, however, this would require major transformations of the EU itself. As I argue later, there is a strong case for replacing the prevalent free market utopia with socially responsible global-Keynesian institutions and policies, and to increase rather than decrease the autonomy of various parts of the whole.

The idea of a pluralistic security community is closely related (cf. Deutsch et al. 1957; Lijphart 1981; Adler and Barnett 1998; Patomäki 2002, ch 8). A security community is defined by the mutually shared understanding that there is an institutionalized capacity to resolve social conflicts through means of peaceful changes. One indication is that actors do not prepare for the use of violence against others, but this is as much an effect as a cause. What matters is that actors accept pluralism and expect peaceful changes to be possible. This means that things do not have to stand as they are now; the status quo is not a norm to be accepted without question.

There is no point in just condemning one or the other side of violent conflicts. The EU–Russia conflict is a tragedy, where neither side wants the outcome, "but at the same time both have been unable to alter the policies that have contributed to the problem in the first place" (Forsberg and Haukkala 2016, 1, also 226). What is required is a perspective that transcends this clash of principles. The problem lies in the implicit fundamentalisms of many political ideologies, neoliberalism included – it does not seem to be easy to accept and live up to the ethos of critical responsiveness (Connolly 1995). As I will argue later, global democracy can provide a desirable way to tackle the concerns of Russian nationalists, Eurasianists and other pluralists in our interconnected world. Democracy is a process whereby conflicts are resolved by peaceful means, and whereby different understandings and purposes are accepted and even cultivated.

Democracy, peaceful changes and security communities are closely connected, although their relationship is complex and can at times be ambiguous. These considerations point toward cosmopolitan democracy understood as a process rather than a model (see Patomäki 2003; Held and Patomäki 2006). Overcoming both double standards and false universalisms would require new global institutional frameworks of dialogue and cooperation, based on the principles of pluralism and comprehensive accountability. The latter should preclude double standards and be grounded on a global rule of law.

Hence, peace requires global democratization and pluralization, especially in the governance of the world economy. The neoliberal era is drawing to a close. The problem is that given the disintegrative tendencies in the global political economy, the transformation to a new era may come only after a global military disaster.

Notes

1 This is complex: for instance, the European Monetary System developed in response to the increasing instability of the re-emerging global ▢ ▢ ▢ ▢system. The idea was to increase stability in Europe. However, the principles of the EMU were rooted in the new classical macroeconomics and the rational expectations theory of Barro, Lucas, Sargent and Wallace, and others, and so the EMU came to be predicated on free market theory with implications for the role of ▢ ▢ ▢ ▢ ▢ ▢ ▢ ▢ ▢, which created actual grounds for instability.
2 The term "good governance" emerged in the late 1980s in the development discourse of the IMF and World Bank. The original idea was to promote smaller, better government. The term "governance", substituted for "government", is closely associated with New Public Management theories of public administration, though its meaning is variable. The dominant meaning aligns with privatization and market-led growth and presupposes a simple Rostowian modernization process. But the term can also assume meanings from political liberalism ("promoting liberal democracy") and various more critical or republican traditions ("promoting participatory development" and ▢ ▢ ▢ ▢ corruption"), though typically rendered compatible with neoliberalism. For analysis see Patomäki (1999a).
3 Sachs (2012) provides *ex post* ▢ ▢ ▢ ▢ ▢ for his role: "I am very proud for what I was able to do, and of my integrity and perseverance in the face of arduous obstacles. Bolivia and Poland achieved historic gains, and I certainly helped in that. Russia, alas, did much more poorly than I had hoped. This note tries to account for that shortfall in the outcomes of Russia's early reforms." Sachs continues: "Dismantling the Soviet-era system seemed to be a mission of great moral rightness. I certainly hoped, and rather expected, that Russia would feel a wave of elation at the new freedom. In this I was somewhat mistaken. The period of elation was remarkably short, and the period of political civility was even shorter."
4 Growth and Gini index ▢ ▢ ▢ from World Bank data, available at http://data.worldbank.org/.

EU, Russia and the conflict in Ukraine 63

5 As we reported first hand, based on a large number of interviews in Moscow, Little Novgorod and St. Petersburg, in Patomäki and Pursiainen (1998).
6 In the 1990s, EU expansion was taken less seriously in Russia. The EU was mostly viewed as a technical conduit for trade. Knowledge about the EU was limited. However, the potential for conflict between the EU and Russia already existed, since the EU represented standard universalizing, Western liberalism in the areas of human rights and democracy; and neoliberalism in economic policy etc. (Patomäki 1996)
7 Panarin was the most articulate Eurasianist theorist in the 1990s, stressing the importance of the military/space-industrial complex. Panarin highlighted politico-economic practices in the West intended to exclude Russia. Panarin also argued that the West accepts and respects multiculturalism but only at the level of "culturological knowledge", whilst also acting as an authoritarian structure reacting aggressively when non-Western nations insist upon their own national values. Accordingly, civilizational pluralism and a creative dialogue of world cultures is possible only in a multipolar world, where the West does not have hegemony. "The mission of Russia is to further multipolarity by creating a counterbalance to the monocentrism rooted in the power of the United States." These ideas are accompanied by systematic criticism of Western culture, not only in terms of its materialism and lack of spirituality, but also in terms of its internal dynamic towards a new kind of "irresponsible, hedonistic individualism" and postmodernism that involves a "neofreudian proletariat", "revolting against the Father", thereby destroying the common, shared civil society by breaking up "the political nation" (see Patomäki and Pursiainen 1998, 24–32, 1999, 68–73).
8 There is a long-standing dispute about whether NATO's expansion into Eastern Europe violated commitments made during the negotiations over German reunification. Russian leaders have accused the West of breaking promises made after the fall of the Iron Curtain. *Der Spiegel* argued in 2009 that "newly discovered documents from Western archives support the Russian position" (see Klußmann, Schepp, and Wiegrefe 2009).
9 Even before the 2007–2008 elections, there was talk in Russia about the danger of a "colour revolution". Academic analysts have been torn between two different interpretations. Some argue that securitization has served Putin's regime in domestic politics, whereas others think that the anxiety of leading Russian politicians is genuine (Duncan 2013). The fear seems genuine, but do the dominant beliefs in Russia conflate concerns about the ruling elite's position and the interests of society at large? It is worth noting that White and McAllister (2014) consider the possibility that Russia barely avoided a "Facebook Revolution" in 2011, though given Putin's popularity in Russia, a genuine "revolution" was unlikely. A new phase in securitization was reached in 2013–2014. Since Ukraine's Euromaidan, Russian leadership has framed mass anti-regime protests at home and abroad as a military threat (Bouchet 2016).
10 Davies (1962, 8) presupposes a variation on Maslow's (1943) hierarchy of needs theory: "A revolutionary state of mind requires the continued, even habitual but dynamic expectation of greater opportunity to satisfy basic needs, which may range from merely physical (food, clothing, shelter, health, and safety from bodily harm) to social (the affectional ties of family and friends) to the need for equal dignity and justice."
11 Unemployment rose to 10% early 2014, but has not been the most important source of poverty in independent Ukraine (a different situation than is "normal"

within the OECD), though insecurities related to unemployment are never just economic but also moral and social, and 2015–2016 unemployment benefit was only 50 USD per month. In GDP terms, there was a partial recovery in Ukraine 2010–2011, but 2012–2015 GDP contracted again, first modestly and then sharply. These developments preceded the political crisis associated with the demonstrations and riots of late 2013 and early 2014. By the end of 2015 the GDP of Ukraine had contracted to its 2005 level.

12 Guzzini (2011) examines securitization as a non-positivistically conceived causal mechanism. For a more future-oriented analysis, making an explicit link between political economy and security, see Patomäki (2015). Aho (1990) summaries the deep-structural and Manichaean underpinnings of the processes of enemy-construction, based partly on his studies of right-wing extremist movements in the United States.
13 Phase 1 should be seen as a generic variety of the process described in Figure 2.1 of Chapter 2.
14 Euro crisis rescue packages devised by the EU and IMF, following the model previously imposed on developing countries, specify public spending cuts to halt deficit increases, but this tends to make public debt a larger share of a contracted or slower economy, requiring then further cuts. Packages may also include: tax reductions to private firms that increase the state burden, retrenchment on public services and distribution policies, wage and pension cuts, and changing labour laws under the euphemism of "flexibility" or "flexicurity" typically involving heightened insecurity and wage cuts, reducing purchasing power and likely aggregate effective demand (Patomäki 2013, ch 4).
15 It is possible that few involved would have accepted the "potential civil war" characterization: principal actors focused on legitimacy, some in terms of popular will, some in terms of the existing law and prevailing order. In general, the meaning and identity of an event or episode is constituted by multiple interpretative perspectives, which when they clash may be akin to a Hobbesian state of war (although war is also a social construction and institution).
16 For points of view, see chapter 7, "Results", of the Wikipedia article "Crimean status referendum, 2014".
17 World Bank data, available at http://data.worldbank.org/.
18 "Putin's Approval Rating Is Down – to 80%", Bloomberg 26 May 2016.
19 This is a TASS news item, 2 March 2017, "Poll shows Putin's approval skyrockets to record high for 2017".

References

Adler, Emmanuel, and Michael Barnett, eds. 1998. *Security Communities*. Cambridge: Cambridge University Press.
Afesorgbor, Sylvanus Kwaku, and Renu Mahadevan. 2016. "The Impact of Economic Sanctions on Income Inequality of Target States." *World Development* 83 (1): 1–11.
Aho, James. 1990. "Heroism, the Construction of Evil, and Violence." In *European Values in International Relations*, edited by Vilho Harle, 15–28. London: Pinter.
Arestis, Philip, Andrew Brown, and Malcolm Sawyer. 2002. "Critical Realism and the Political Economy of the Euro." Working Paper No. 352, Levy Economics

Institute, New York. www.levyinstitute.org/publications/critical-realism-and-the-political-economy-of-the-euro.
Ashley, Richard K. 1989. "Imposing International Purpose: Notes on a Problematic of Governance." In *Global Changes and Theoretical Challenges*, edited by Ernst-Otto Czempiel and James N. Rosenau, 251–90. Lexington: Lexington Books.
Barkawi, Tarak, and Mark Laffey. 1999. "The Imperial Peace: Democracy, Force and Globalization." *European Journal of International Relations* 5 (4): 403–34.
Biersteker, Thomas. 2014. "Dialectical Reflections on Transformations of Global Security during the Long Twentieth Century." *Globalizations* 11 (5): 711–31.
Bogdan, Tetiana, and Michael Landesmann. 2017. *From Fiscal Austerity towards Growth-Enhancing Fiscal Policy in Ukraine*. Research Report 417. Vienna: The Vienna Institute for International Economic Studies. https://wiiw.ac.at/from-fiscal-austerity-towards-growth-enhancing-fiscal-policy-in-ukraine-dlp-4189.pdf.
Bouchet, Nicolas. 2016. "Russia's 'Militarization' of Colour Revolutions: Since Ukraine's EuroMaidan, Russia Sees Mass Anti-Regime Protests at Home and Abroad as a Military Threat." *CSS Policy Perspectives* 4 (2), January. www.css.ethz.ch/content/dam/ethz/special-interest/gess/cis/center-for-securities-studies/pdfs/PP4-2.pdf.
Chandler, David, and Julian Reid. 2016. *The Neoliberal Subject: Resilience, Adaptation and Vulnerability*. London and New York: Rowman & Littlefield.
Connolly, William E. 1995. *The Ethos of Pluralization*. Minneapolis: University of Minnesota Press.
Cordesman, Anthony H. 2014. "Russia and the 'Color Revolution'": A Russian Military View of a World Destabilized by the US and the West." *CSIS Center for Strategic and International Studies*, May 28. www.csis.org/analysis/russia-and-%E2%80%9Ccolor-revolution%E2%80%9D.
Cremona, Marise, and Christophe Hillion. 2006. "L'Union fait la force? Potential and Limitations of the European Neighbourhood Policy as an Integrated EU Foreign and Security Policy." EUI Working Papers No. 2006/39, Department of Law, San Domenico di Fiesole. http://cadmus.eui.eu/bitstream/handle/1814/6419/LAW-2006-39.pdf.
Dafoe, Allan, John R. Oneal, and Bruce Russett. 2013. "The Democratic Peace: Weighing the Evidence and Cautious Inference." *International Studies Quarterly* 57 (1): 201–14.
Davies, James C. 1962. "Toward a Theory of Revolution." *American Sociological Review* 27 (1): 5–19.
Delcour, Laure. 2017. *The EU and Russia in Their 'Contested Neighbourhood': Multiple External Influences, Policy Transfer and Domestic Change*. London: Routledge.
Delcour, Laure, and Kataryna Wolczuk. 2015. "Spoiler or Facilitator of Democratization? Russia's Role in Georgia and Ukraine." *Democratization* 22 (3): 459–78.
Deutsch, Karl W. 1963. *The Nerves of Government: Models of Political Communication and Control*. New York: The Free Press.
Deutsch, Karl W., Sidney A. Burrell, Robert A. Kann, Maurice Lee, Jr., Martin Lichterman, Raymond E. Lindgren, Francis L. Loewenheim, and Richard W. Van Wagenen. 1957. *Political Community and the North Atlantic Area: International*

Organization in the Light of Historical Experience. Princeton: Princeton University Press.
Doyle, Michael W. 1983a. "Kant, Liberal Legacies, and Foreign Affairs, Part I." *Philosophy and Public Affairs* 12 (3): 205–35.
Doyle, Michael W. 1983b. "Kant, Liberal Legacies, and Foreign Affairs, Part II." *Philosophy and Public Affairs* 12 (4): 323–53.
Doyle, Michael W. 1986. "Liberalism and World Politics." *American Political Science Review* 80 (4): 1151–69.
Doyle, Michael W. 2005. "Three Pillars of the Liberal Peace." *American Political Science Review* 99 (3): 463–6.
Drezner, Daniel W. (2015) "Targeted Sanctions in a World of Global Finance." *International Interactions: Empirical and Theoretical Research in International Relations* 41 (4): 755–64.
Duncan, Peter J. S. 2013. "Russia, the West and the 2007–2008 Electoral Cycle: Did the Kremlin Really Fear a 'Coloured Revolution'?" *Europe-Asia Studies* 65 (1): 1–25.
Eagleton-Pierce, Matthew. 2016. *Neoliberalism: The Key Concepts*. London: Routledge.
EU. 2016. "Shared Vision, Common Action: A Stronger Europe." *A Global Strategy for the European Union's Foreign and Security Policy*. Brussels, June. https://europa.eu/globalstrategy/en/shared-vision-common-action-stronger-europe.
EU (European Union). European Commission. 2004. *Communication from the Commission: European Neighbourhood Policy: Strategy Paper*. COM (2004) 373 Final, Brussels, May 12. http://eur-lex.europa.eu/legal-content/EN/TXT/PDF/?uri=CELEX:52004DC0373&from=en.
Forsberg, Tuomas, and Hiski Haukkala. 2016. *The European Union and Russia*. London: Palgrave.
Fukuyama, Francis (1989) "The End of History." *The National Interest* (16 Summer 1989): 3–18.
Galtung, Johan. 1969. "Violence, Peace, and Peace Research." *Journal of Peace Research* 6 (3): 167–91.
Galtung, Johan. 1973. *The European Community: A Superpower in the Making*. London (Universitetsforlaget: Oslo): George Allen & Unwin.
Gordon, Joy. 2016. "Economic Sanctions as 'Negative Development': The Case of Cuba." *Journal of International Development* 28 (4): 473–84.
Guzzini, Stefano. 2011. "Securitization as a Causal Mechanism." *Security Dialogue* 42 (4–5): 329–41.
Habermas, Jürgen. 1988. *Legitimation Crisis*. Translated by Thomas McCarthy. Cambridge: Polity Press.
Hafner, Reeta. 2015. "Reshaping Enmity: Studying Change in the Relations between the Islamic Republic of Iran and the United States of America." MA diss., World Politics, Faculty of Social Sciences, University of Helsinki. https://helda.helsinki.fi/handle/10138/158704?show=full.
Held, David, and Heikki Patomäki. 2006. "Problems of Global Democracy: A Dialogue." *Theory, Culture & Society* 23 (5): 115–33.
Huntington, Samuel P. 1991. "Democracy's Third Wave." *Journal of Democracy* 2 (2): 12–34.

Jones, Lee. 2015. *Societies Under Siege: Exploring How International Economic Sanctions (Do Not) Work*. Oxford: Oxford University Press.

Khan, Haider, and Heikki Patomäki. 2010. "A Reconstructive Critique of IPE and GPE from a Critical Scientific Realist Perspective: An Alternative Keynesian-Kaleckian Approach." Paper presented in panel WD24 at the ISA 51st Convention, New Orleans, LA, February 17–20.

Kindleberger, Charles. 2000. *Manias, Panics, and Crashes: A History of Financial Crises*. 4th ed. New York: John Wiley & Sons.

Klußmann, Uwe, Matthias Schepp, and Klaus Wiegrefe. 2009. "NATO's Eastward Expansion: Did the West Break Its Promise to Moscow?" *Der Spiegel*, November 26. www.spiegel.de/international/world/nato-s-eastward-expansion-did-the-west-break-its-promise-to-moscow-a-663315.html.

Krugman, Paul. 1979. "Increasing Returns, Monopolistic Competition, and International Trade." *Journal of International Economics* 9 (4): 469–79.

Krugman, Paul. 1980. "Scale Economies, Product Differentiation, and the Pattern of Trade." *The American Economic Review* 70 (5): 950–9.

Krugman, Paul. 1981. "Intraindustry Specialisation and the Gains from Trade." *The Journal of Political Economy* 89 (5): 959–73.

Kuchins, Andrew, and Igor Zevelev. 2012. "Russia's Contested National Identity and Foreign Policy." In *Worldviews of Aspiring Powers: Domestic Foreign Policy Debates in China, India, Iran, Japan, and Russia*, edited by Henry R. Nau and Deepa Ollapally, 181–209. Oxford: Oxford University Press.

Kurki, Milja. 2012. *Democratic Futures: Re-Visioning Democracy Promotion*. London: Routledge.

Lees, Nicholas. 2013. "Structural Inequality, Quasi-Rents and the Democratic Peace: A Neo-Ricardian Analysis of International Order." *Millennium: Journal of International Studies* 41 (3): 491–515.

Lijphart, Arend. 1981. "Karl W. Deutsch and the New Paradigm in International Relations." In *From National Development to Global Community: Essays in Honour of Karl W. Deutsch*, edited by Richard L. Merritt and Bruce Russett, 233–51. Boston: Allen and Unwin.

List, Friedrich. (1841) 1885. *The National System of Political Economy*. Translated by Sampson S. Lloyd, 1885. http://oll.libertyfund.org/titles/list-the-national-system-of-political-economy.

Markwell, Donald. 2006. *John Maynard Keynes and International Relations: Economic Paths to Peace*. Oxford: Oxford University Press.

Marx, Karl. (1847) 2008. "Moralizing Criticism and Critical Morality: A Polemic against Karl Heinzen." In *Selected Essays*, 79–98. Charleston: Bibliobazaar.

Maslow, Abraham H. 1943. "A Theory of Human Motivation." *Psychological Review* 50 (4): 370–96.

Minsky, Hyman (2008) *Stabilizing an Unstable Economy*. New York: McGraw Hill.

Morgan, T. Clifton. 2015. "Hearing the Noise: Economic Sanctions Theory and Anomalous Evidence." *International Interactions* 41 (4): 744–54.

Morgenthau, Hans J. 1948. *Politics among Nations: The Struggle for Power and Peace*. New York: Alfred A. Knopf.

Moser, John E. 2016. *The Global Great Depression and the Coming of World War II*. London: Routledge.
Mousseau, Michael. 2003. "The Nexus of Market Society, Liberal Preferences, and Democratic Peace: Interdisciplinary Theory and Evidence." *International Studies Quarterly* 47 (4): 486–510.
Mousseau, Michael, Håvard Hegre, and John R. Oneal. 2003. "How the Wealth of Nations Conditions the Liberal Peace." *European Journal of International Relations* 9 (2): 277–314.
Mueller, John. 1970. "Presidential Popularity from Truman to Johnson." *American Political Science Review* 64 (1): 18–34.
Ohlin, Bertil. (1933) 1952. *Interregional and International Trade*. Harvard Economic Studies Vol. 39, Cambridge: Harvard University Press.
Patomäki, Heikki. 1996. *Vain kauppakumppaneita? EU, Venäjä ja EU:n ulkosuhteiden rakenteistuminen* [Only Trading Partners? EU, Russia and the Structuration of the External Relations of the EU]. Helsinki: UPI (Haasteita 11).
Patomäki, Heikki, and Christer Pursiainen (1999) "Western Models and the Russian Idea: Beyond Inside/Outside in the Discourses on Civil Society." *Millennium: Journal of International Studies* 28 (1): 53–77.
Patomäki, Heikki. 1999a. "Good Governance of the World Economy?" *Alternatives* 24 (1): 119–42.
Patomäki, Heikki. 1999b. "Western Models and the Russian Idea: Beyond Inside/Outside in the Discourses on Civil Society." *Millennium: Journal of International Studies* 28 (1): 53–77.
Patomäki, Heikki. 2002. *After International Relations: Critical Realism and the (Re)construction of World Politics*. London: Routledge.
Patomäki, Heikki. 2003. "Problems of Democratising Global Governance: Time, Space and the Emancipatory Process." *European Journal of International Relations* 9 (3): 347–76.
Patomäki, Heikki (2013) *The Great Eurozone Disaster: From Crisis to Global New Deal*. London & New York: Zed Books.
Patomäki, Heikki (2015) "Absenting the Absence of Future Dangers and Structural Transformations in Securitization Theory." *International Relations* 29 (1): 128–136.
Patomäki, Heikki. 2016a. "International Political Economy and Security." In *The Routledge Handbook of Security Studies*. 2nd ed., edited by Thierry Balzacq and Myriam Dunn Cavelty, 32–42. London: Routledge.
Patomäki, Heikki. 2016b. "Democracy in a Globalized World." In *International Relations Theory Today*, edited by Ken Booth and Toni Erskine, 190–201. Cambridge: Polity Press.
Patomäki, Heikki, and Christer Pursiainen. 1998. "Against the State, with(in) the State or a Transnational Creation: Russian Civil Society in the Making." Working Papers No. 4, UPI (FIIA – the Finnish Institute for International Affairs), Helsinki.
Peksen, Dursun, and A. Cooper Drury. 2010. "Coercive or Corrosive: The Negative Impact of Economic Sanctions on Democracy." *International Interactions* 36 (3): 240–64.
Piketty, Thomas. 2014. *Capital in the Twenty-First Century*. Translated by Arthur Goldhammer. Cambridge: The Belknap Press (of Harvard University Press).

Pinker, Steven. 2011. *The Better Angels of Our Nature: The Decline of Violence in History and Its Causes*. London: Allen Lane.
Polanyi, Karl. (1944) 2001. *The Great Transformation: The Political and Economic Consequences of Our Time*. Boston: Beacon Press.
Ray, James Lee. 2013. "War on Democratic Peace." *International Studies Quarterly* 57 (1): 198–200.
Ricardo, David. 1821. *Principles of Political Economy and Taxation*. 3rd ed. London: John Murray. www.econlib.org/library/Ricardo/ricP.html.
Rosato, Sebastian. 2003. "The Flawed Logic of Democratic Peace Theory." *American Political Science Review* 97 (4): 585–602.
Sachs, Jeffrey. 2012. "What I Did in Russia." *Jeffrey Sachs Blog*, March 14. http://jeffsachs.org/2012/03/what-i-did-in-russia/.
Sakwa, Richard. 2016. *Frontline Ukraine: Crisis in the Borderlands*. London: I.B. Tauris.
Sayer, Andrew. 2009. *The Moral Significance of Class*. Cambridge: Cambridge University Press.
Schneider, Gerald. 2014. "Peace through Globalization and Capitalism? Prospects of Two Liberal Propositions." *Journal of Peace Research* 51 (2): 173–83.
Shahabi, Shohreh, Hooman Fazlalizadeh, Jennifer Stedman, Linus Chuang, Ahmad Shariftabrizi, and Regina Ram. 2015. "The Impact of International Economic Sanctions on Iranian Cancer Healthcare." *Health Policy* 119 (10): 1309–18.
Shirreff, Richard. 2016. *2017: A War with Russia*. London: Coronet (an imprint of Hodder & Stoughton).
von Soest, Christian, and Michael Wahman. 2015. "Are Democratic Sanctions Really Counterproductive?" *Democratization* 22 (6): 957–80.
Wang, Wan. 2015. "Impact of Western Sanctions on Russia in the Ukraine Crisis." *Journal of Politics and Law* 8 (2): 1–6.
Wendt, Alexander. 1999. *Social Theory of International Politics*. Cambridge: Cambridge University Press.
White, Stephen, and Ian McAllister. 2014. "Did Russia (Nearly) Have a Facebook Revolution in 2011? Social Media's Challenge to Authoritarianism." *Politics* 34 (1): 72–84.

4 Trumponomics and the logic of global disintegration

Like Brexit, the election of Donald Trump can be tentatively explained using Polanyi's double movement (Pettifor 2017). The US has been leading the project of liberal globalization since World War II and was largely responsible in the 1970s for the unilateral shift from Bretton Woods embedded liberalism (Ruggie 1982) to neoliberalism. Subsequent decades have had far-reaching effects on income, wealth and power distributions in the US, enriching a "1%". Moreover, it is widely acknowledged that the US has become less democratic and its political system increasingly captive to powerful business interests (e.g. Putnam 2001; APSA Task Force 2004; Palast 2004; Wolin 2010; Stiglitz 2013). These developments have resonated with systematic attempts to detach markets and corporations from democratic regulation.

In this reading, Trump emerged as the leader of those left behind, attracting supporters from all social classes. Ordinary US wage-earners are anxious to sustain what they consider to be the normal standard of living. They are working significantly longer and are more involved in debt than their parents previously were (e.g. Chernomas and Hudson 2017, 36–44). One indicator is the spread of anxiety disorders and depression. Image and status anxiety are closely related to what and whom people appear to be and think they are in a society of materialist values that judges by looks, position, wealth and social background.[1]

Larger differences in material circumstances create greater social distances, increasing feelings of superiority and inferiority. This is one of the key reasons why mental illness and drug abuse correlate strongly with the level of inequality (Pickett and Wilkinson 2010, 63–72). Unemployment seems especially important in explaining class-based differences in mental illness (Richards and Paskov 2016). This accords with the hypothesis that there is an intrinsic relation between uncertainty generated by labour market uncertainties and anxiety. Predictably, after the global financial crisis of 2008–2009, "many experienced the economic system as threatening to their life chances, their incomes, their futures, and their way of life." (Pettifor 2017, 44) Citing Polanyi's contention that modern nationalism is a protective reaction, Ann Pettifor explains that

> As Karl Polanyi predicted, these societies, in a 'counter-movement' to globalisation and recognising the failure of democratic governments to protect societies from the depredations of self-regulating markets, have reacted by electing 'strong men' (and women) that do offer protection. Donald Trump posed as a strong protector, and won the support of those Americans 'left behind' by globalisation.
>
> (Pettifor 2017, 53)

A major problem for this Polanyian explanation is that Trump, like UKIP, is not critical of markets as such but rather criticizes specific others for unfair or unpatriotic behaviour. If the point is to protect society against self-regulating markets, why should Trump's voters then approve his selective but sweeping pro-market reforms, such as major public spending cuts, financial deregulation and tax concessions to corporations and very wealthy individuals?

A closer look at the context of many US voters reveals that support for Trump stems not only from the prevailing common sense and false or misleading beliefs, but also stems from an informed but disillusioned response to power disparities and double standards within the US. What is likewise interesting is that although the convergence of social forces in the US seems similar to developments in the UK, the US constellation of political forces is more lop-sided. In the 2016 election a large majority of the US economic and political elite either stood behind Hillary Clinton or found Trump's popularity puzzling.

The rise of Trump has led many in Washington, New York and other major centres to fear for the future of the neoliberal world order. The German magazine *Der Spiegel* warned January 2017 that the US is withdrawing from global politics: "Russia's annexation of Crimea was the first indication that the global order that we had enjoyed for 25 years was under threat." As a consequence of Trump, "the collapse of the old world order" is now benefitting countries like Russia and China (Der Spiegel 2017). Many perceive Trump to be a threat to the global liberal system of values and practices.[2] The US seems to be giving up its leadership, with possibly detrimental consequences for the whole world system.

This reaction accords with the basic ideas of hegemonic stability theory (HST), positing that a single hegemonic state is a both a necessary and a sufficient condition for an open, liberal world economy and related security system. A similar response was evident in the literature of the 1970s and

1980s concerning the perceived "decline" of US global hegemonic power at the time (acutely analysed by Strange 1987; Grunberg 1990). However, this was partly, and temporarily, set aside by the end of the Cold War and during the "roaring nineties" (Stiglitz 2003) and its aftermath, when American exceptionalism gained ground. This aftermath finally ended in the global financial crisis 2008–2009. Since then, some pundits have started to argue "this time it's real" (e.g. Layne 2012; for discussion see Wohlforth 2012).

In this chapter, I first discuss the causes of Trump's election in more detail. The main focus of this chapter is, however, on the disintegrative consequences of Trump (or, if Trump fails, on the likely consequences of the social dispositions and shifts that made his presidency possible). I argue that apparent breaks and novelties notwithstanding, in many ways Trump represents an intensification of tendencies that long preceded his presidency. To clarify these continuities, I outline the logic of hegemonic stability theory and expose its normative underpinnings and ambiguities.

I then discuss the issue of whether global cooperation is possible "after hegemony", as argued by Keohane in 1984 (2005), one of the original authors of hegemonic stability theory. According to Keohane, while a hegemonic state may facilitate the emergence and development of common institutions, they may well continue to exist and function after hegemony in a decentralized way, through extended, bendable and institutionally ensured tit-for-tat strategies. The obvious problem from this point of view is that if the former hegemon refuses to cooperate, it can lead to a spiral of tit-for-tat retaliations. I try to show the limitations of this economistic literature and discuss alternative conceptualizations of hegemony and the politics of global cooperation. The global common good is profoundly contested in both theory and practice. How it should be seen depends on our factual and normative theories of political economy and peace and security.

Finally, I argue that a dialectical perspective on change and continuity in world history can be a powerful analytical tool for understanding the causes and consequences of the present global conjuncture and potential crises. The appearance of stability and of fixedness in the international "order" is more of an illusion than a reality. From a dialectical point of view, events are understood as multiple contradictory and complementary layers, often involving inner determinations "to which they own their hidden unities, divergent meanings, and possible futures" (Alker et al. 1996, 351). Thus HST, under current historical circumstances, may function to justify, and thus co-generate, Trump's approach to US trade and security policies. When weaker states are perceived to free ride on the US, in the new US administration's view it is apparently only fair that the US should apply countervailing measures, either to balance its current account or to compel others to pay the costs for the military burden of defending them.

The "hegemonic stability" of the liberal-capitalist world economy is a specific but not the only model for world order. World order models constitute those doctrines of practical action and institutional design that exist, reign, cooperate, compete and at times clash in any given geo-historical era. Doctrines codify the lessons learned from previous practices; and doctrinal debates define geo-historical eras and their characteristic practical and institutional arrangements. Collective learning and the exercise of power (understood as transformative capacity), not least by social movements, determine which doctrines prevail. What exactly does Trumponomics, the economic policies of his administration, mean for the project of neoliberal globalization? What new doctrines are emerging, if any, and what would be the rational direction of world history?

Explaining the outcome of US 2016 elections

In any election, voters for X can be divided into subgroups in terms of what the decisive issues or reasons for that vote were. If a subgroup is bigger than the margin by which X won, then the issues and reasons especially important for that subgroup can be singled out as "the cause" of the victory. From this perspective, a few hundred thousand US voters decided the outcome of the US presidential elections of 2016. It is unsurprising there are multiple incompatible explanations concerning the victory of Trump 8 November 2016.

This approach cannot explain why Trump rose against all odds to be Republican candidate, or why Bernie Sanders came close to the Democratic candidacy (receiving 39% of the vote). We need an account of the main trends and tendencies. The Chapter 2 analysis is applicable here: the roles of media, money and structural relations of power are important in the formation of a hegemonic common sense. Human actors assemble familiar meanings that are constitutive of the prevailing "common sense", which media both responds to and serves to construct in complex ways. Social causation requires actors and actions, and action includes the possibility of doing otherwise. Citizens can change their minds, particularly in view of topical events or new framings or pieces of information, and the overall composition of the electorate fluctuates. The opinions of others, and overall "public opinion" so often cited or made to talk in public debates, is intertwined with actors' own will-formation.

The political economy background of the 2016 election is well known. The rise of inequality in the US is illustrated in Figures 4.1 and 4.2. Since the late 1970s, increased labour productivity in the United States has mainly benefitted higher income levels. The proportion of national product comprised by capital has risen markedly, and the proportion of the total accounted for

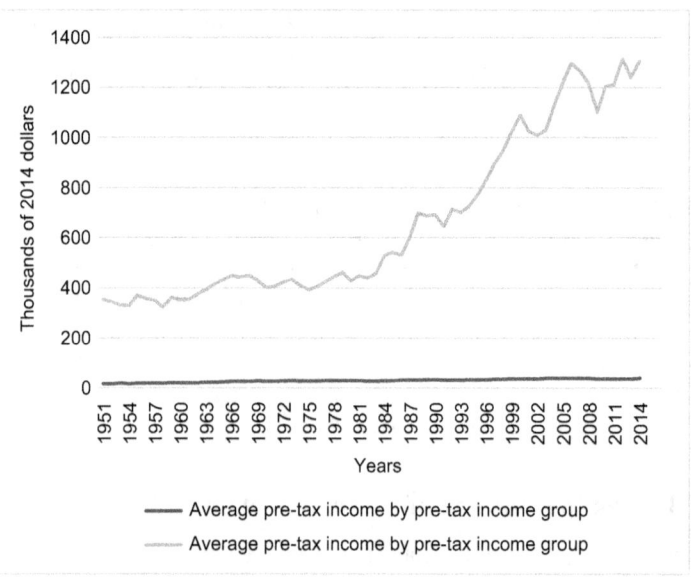

Figure 4.1 Income inequality: top 1 percent and bottom 90 percent average pre-tax incomes, 1949–2014

Source: Data from Thomas Piketty, Emmanuel Saez, and Gabriel Zucman, 2016, *Distributional National Accounts: Methods and Estimates for the United States*, Data Appendix, tables II, B3, http://piketty.pse.ens.fr/files/PSZ2016DataAppendix.pdf.

Figure 4.2 Wealth inequality: top 1 percent and bottom 90 percent average wealth, 1949–2014

Source: Data from Thomas Piketty, Emmanuel Saez, and Gabriel Zucman, 2016, *Distributional National Accounts: Methods and Estimates for the United States*, Data Appendix, tables II, E3, http://piketty.pse.ens.fr/files/PSZ2016DataAppendix.pdf.

by labour has dropped from 60 to below 50% (still including the salaries of top management). The average hourly pay of regular employees peaked around 1973, and since then wage levels have generally stagnated and in some categories fallen. After the global financial crisis, partly caused by rising inequalities and American households' involvement in debt,[3] these developments intensified. From 2009 to 2015, the wealthiest 1% of Americans captured 52% of total real-income growth (Saez 2016, 5–6).

Both Trump and Sanders were critical from outside the established concerns of their respective parties. Sanders focused directly on campaign finance reform and income and wealth inequality, which he argued eroded the American middle class. Trump promised to rebuild infrastructure, make American industry more competitive by nationalist means and return well-paying manufacturing jobs to the US. Each addressed similar anxieties but in different ways: Sanders stressed the importance of progressive taxation and universal healthcare and education, whereas Trump promised to use the federal state to protect American industrial interests and thereby make well-paying jobs available again to ordinary wage-earners. Both were critical of at least some free trade agreements. Sanders's platform appealed especially to younger and black voters (similar to "Remain" in the UK 2016 referendum), Trump to older and white voters (like "Leave" in the UK).

Trump was particularly popular in the parts of the US that experienced a continued loss of jobs, whether because of globalization or automation or both. Figure 4.3 describes the GDP value added share of manufacturing

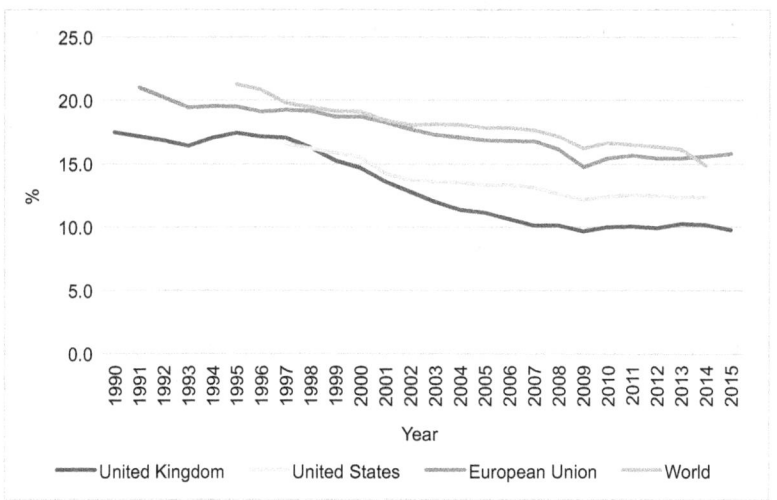

Figure 4.3 Manufacturing, value added (% of GDP)

Source: Data from World Bank, *World development Indicators*, at http://data.worldbank.org/indicator/NV.IND.MANF.ZS?locations=US-GB-1W-EU.

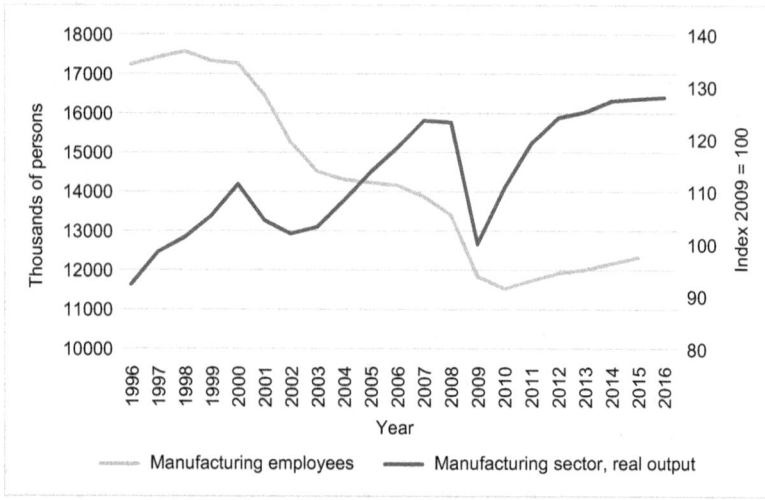

Figure 4.4 Manufacturing employees and real output

Sources: Data from U.S. Bureau of Labor Statistics, retrieved from FRED, Federal Reserve Bank of St. Louis. https://fred.stlouisfed.org/series/MANEMP; and https://fred.stlouisfed.org/series/OUTMS, May 9, 2017; U.S. Bureau of Labor Statistics, retrieved from FRED, Federal Reserve Bank of St. Louis; https://fred.stlouisfed.org/series/OUTMS, May 9, 2017.

(world, US, EU and UK). This share has been declining in all cases, but nonetheless, in 2016 and in absolute terms, the US was manufacturing more than ever before. Figure 4.4 illustrates the growing gap between the value of production and employment. This suggests that automation has been more important than relocation in terms of loss of jobs in manufacturing. This does not mean that relocations and globalization are unimportant, but at the national level the main significance of globalization may lie in the way the possibility of relocation has changed power relations between capital and labour.

During campaigning, Trump avoided challenging asymmetric social structures and power relations within the US. According to a common assessment, many of Trump's nationalist–protectionist policies are unlikely to be implemented or succeed, whereas his tax- and other reforms will most benefit the richest 1% and further impoverish lower income strata.[4] In other words, many of those who voted for Trump seem to have voted against their own economic interests. Mayhew summarizes the widespread incredulity concerning US voters' lack of rationality:

> Analysts have puzzled over why voters assumed to be concerned about a loss of jobs were willing to accept the vague and sometimes contra-

dictory prescription that Trump offered as a remedy and why they voted for a man and a party that promise to take apart the existing safety net.

(Mayhew 2017, 29)

Mayhew argues that there are many areas in the US where Tea Party anger is strong but jobs not necessarily lacking and the living standards about the US average. These people are protesting against the ruling urban elite and their sense of superiority and double standards. The federal state had lost legitimacy in their eyes because they "had reached a not unreasonable conclusion that regulation was applied to them but not to the big firms" (32). Regulations seem biased against the common people. In the absence of feasible alternatives, voters may thus appear, for example, anti-environmentalist, although their main concern is the future of the place where they are living and the local community to which they belong.

Members of modern societies are vulnerable to generalized anxiety when their relations are mediated only through impersonal markets and bureaucratic regulations not of their own making. People whose identity is constituted by a particular place can feel threatened by market and bureaucratic forces that appear to endanger the future of that place. A major economic crisis can make those fears and anxieties acute. Jobs and incomes matter, and there is an intrinsic relation between unemployment-related uncertainty and anxiety, but for many Trump voters the main issues may have been community and a sense of fairness. This of course comes close to the Polanyian explanation: society is trying to protect itself against markets.[5]

Hegemonic stability theory

What, then, are the consequences of Trump to the world economy and its governance? Hegemonic Stability Theory (HST) claims that the stability of the world economy is dependent on the benevolent leadership of the hegemonic state. The US share of exports and world GDP have been declining since the 1950s. The US began to run trade deficits in the late 1950s, and this problem became more serious in the 1960s. HST emerged in the 1970s when the unilateral dismantling of the Bretton Woods system was widely conceived as a sign of crisis in US global leadership. This perception was further reinforced by the ostensibly acute economic troubles of the US, the catastrophe of the Vietnam War and the rise of the New Left movement. The Vietnam War came to an end in 1975 and the New Left seemed to fade away, but the underlying economic developments have continued. The US share of global manufacturing value added has declined over time, from some 30% in the early 1980s to roughly 19% in 2015. Has US leadership come to an end?

HST was first proposed by Kindleberger (1973) in *The World in Depression 1929–1939*. In the concluding chapter of that work, "An Explanation of the 1929 Depression", Kindleberger suggested a chain of partly contrastive historical analogies between three eras. The first was the era of free trade under British leadership from 1846 (the abolition of the Corn Laws) or 1860 (further elimination of tariffs) until 1913.[6] The second was the interwar era of 1919–1939, when the US first refused to accept the role of hegemonic leadership and then resorted to the protectionist Smoot-Hawley Tariff Act of 1930 in response to the financial crisis and its consequences. The third was the era of US (hegemonic) leadership 1945–1971. A fourth era began in the 1970s, when the US was arguably "beginning to slip" (307), but which we retrospectively know as the era of neoliberalism or market globalism (see Harvey 2005; Steger 2009; Springer, Birch, and MacLeavy 2016).

Kindleberger anticipated future tendencies towards protectionism and a diplomatic stalemate between the US and the EEC. The next forty years turned out differently, but in Kindleberger's historical reading, a stalemate and repression implies heightened danger of a regressive spiral into war. These historical analogies and anticipations were subsequently formulated into a general theory by Krasner (1976); Keohane (1980); Gilpin (1981); and Kindleberger (1981) himself. In Krasner's (1976, 318) formulation, the main hypothesis is that "a hegemonic distribution of potential economic power is likely to result in an open trading structure" and, more generally, in an open world economy.

Krasner qualified his state-power argument by talking about delayed political reactions to changes in patterns of trade and finance and structures of production; the actual effects of gradual economic changes may in some cases become visible only after decades. Moreover, "some catalytic external event seems necessary to move states to dramatic policy initiatives in line with state interests" (1976, 341). Policy choices are thus path-dependent, and states quite easily become locked into the pattern set by previous choices. The key assumption underlying the theory of hegemonic stability, however, is that free trade and maximal (global) openness in investments and finance are beneficial to everyone, albeit not equally so, in sharp contrast to many alternative perspectives (Rodrik 2001; Unger 2007):

> Neoclassical trade theory is based upon the assumption that states act to maximize their aggregate economic utility. This leads to the conclusion that maximum global welfare and Pareto optimality are achieved under free trade. While particular countries may better their situations through protectionism, economic theory has generally looked askance at such policies. [. . .] Neoclassical theory recognizes that trade regulations can also be used to correct domestic distortions and to promote

infant industries, but these are exceptions or temporary departures from policy conclusions that lead logically to the support of free trade.

(Krasner 1976, 318)

Krasner stressed that the benefits are clearest in the case of large and technologically advanced states and for some small states, but large backward states may in some cases experience excessive costs from trade openness. Krasner's qualifications notwithstanding, the liberal international order was bluntly defined as a (global) public good in the next step of the development of the theory. The global public good was supposed to include the definition and enforcement of property rights, resolution of disputes, stability and security (Gilpin 1981, 16, 30, 34, 1987, 86–7; Kindleberger 1981, 247). Yet these HST theorists were not united about the nature of what constituted that "good".[7] Whereas Kindleberger emphasized moral responsibilities and the need to overcome temporary asymmetries and counter business cycles, Gilpin, by contrast, put forward a more neo-imperialist interpretation:

> As was the case with premodern empires, the hegemonic powers may be said to supply public goods (security and protection of property rights) in exchange for revenue. The Pax Britannica and Pax Americana, like the Pax Romana, ensured an international system of relative peace and security.
>
> (Gilpin 1981, 145)

The theory of hegemonic stability depicted nineteenth-century Britain as a model for the late twentieth- and early twenty-first-century US. The precise ethical and political implications of the theory were somewhat unclear. Gilpin presented a gloomy picture of future options. Despite the Cold War bipolar structure being a major stabilizing factor, threatened only by the continuous rise of the Soviet Union, Gilpin argued that "the danger of a hegemonic war is very real" (234). His prescription: a hegemonic or imperial enforcement – i.e. that powerful states should control the "lesser states" – for global security and protection of property rights has been taken seriously by many US-based scholars, politicians and journalists. Coupled with the assumption of the benevolence of the hegemon and related apologetic narratives, this line of thinking readily lends itself to the conclusion that the US has been assuming an unfair share of sustaining the global public good. Others are free-riding on the US.[8] Strange expressed the main practical implication of the theory:

> [T]he myth of lost hegemony is apt to induce in everybody only pessimism, despair, and the conviction that, in these inauspicious circum-

stances, the only thing to do is to ignore everyone else and look after your own individual or national interests. [It . . .] may paradoxically be contributing to a less cooperative environment by subscribing to and perpetuating the myth of lost American power.

(Strange 1987, 552)

Trump's project to "make America great again" thus has deep historical roots. The erosion of the Bretton Woods system triggered the emergence of the US-American myth of lost hegemony and its negative global consequences. However, the Bretton Woods system itself was inherently dilemmatic and presupposed the largely disintegrated world economy of the 1940s and its economic domination by the US. The Triffin Dilemma[9] was a direct consequence of the decision reached in Bretton Woods – on the insistence of the US – to make the dollar the currency of world trade, and let creditors retain their surplus and remain passive. The turning point of the early 1970s would not have occurred until much later had Keynes's proposal been implemented in full, and it could have occurred in a different way (Patomäki 2008, 185–90). The implication of HST – that others should be made to pay for the maintenance of the existing "order" and indirectly subsidize the costs on US terms – paved the way for the US to become progressively self-regarding.

Of the early developers of HST, Kindleberger (1973, 308) was open to the alternative of new international institutions with real authority and sovereignty to govern the world economy (i.e. an evolutionary path towards a "post-hegemonic" situation, with increased transnationalization of state authority, governing a highly transnationalized global economic system). However, he too seems to have ultimately assumed that agenda setting and decision-making must always be hierarchical at least to a degree; i.e. one state must always lead and others must follow.

International cooperation "after hegemony": a reconstructive critique

The assumption underlying HST – that a single hegemonic leader is necessary for effective international cooperation (to uphold existing international institutions and ensure the stability of the global capitalist economic system) – was questioned by Keohane 1984 (2005). Here, Keohane (2005) argues, "it might be possible, after the decline of hegemonic regimes, for most symmetrical patterns of cooperation to evolve after a transitional period of discord".

Keohane uses game theory to show that spontaneous cooperation can emerge even among egoists and in the absence of common government, but "the extent of such cooperation will depend on the existence of international institutions, or international regimes, with particular characteristics" (2005, 13). The possibility of continuing effective international cooperation "after hegemony" is reinforced by the complementary nature of hegemony and international regimes. These can make agreement possible, and facilitate continuing compliance with the rules established in the system of world order.

In his analysis, Keohane makes it clear there is no need to expect serious historical decline in international cooperation in the 1980s, 1990s or beyond, even as US dominance within the system gradually declines.

"[The] system" itself will not collapse into a state of chaos or disorder. On the contrary, there is a real prospect that vital post-war international norms, institutions, and practices will not only continue, but will even be strengthened.

(Keohane 2005, 79)

This is a condition he refers to as "non-hegemonic cooperation". Keohane's account rests on a view of states-as-rational-egoists. He concretely considers instances of international cooperation in fields such as monetary policy and the oil sector, as an iterated prisoner's dilemma (PD) game (following Axelrod 1984). He extends his analysis to cover the impact of ethics, power and institutions on international cooperation. According to Keohane, tit-for-tat is the best strategy in an iterated PD-game. Matters are complicated by many players, asymmetric information, moral hazard and irresponsibility, whilst multiple parallel games in issue areas, the unequal nature of inter-state relations (in power terms: only some states really count) and the existence of established international organizations can alleviate these problems.

Thus, intensive interaction among a few players helps to substitute or supplement hegemonic actions. As a hegemon's power erodes, a gradual shift may take place from hegemonic to non-hegemonic cooperation. Increasingly, incentives to cooperate will depend not only on the hegemon's responses but also on those of other sizeable states. Such a transition may be difficult in practice, since expectations may lag behind reality; but nothing in rational choice analysis renders it impossible (Keohane 2005, 79).

Keohane has not been alone in envisaging the possibility of future international cooperation without a single hegemon. Young (1989, 1991) retains the view of states-as-rational-egoists, but also considers various forms of initiative and leadership in creating new regimes of cooperation, including intellectual leadership. Haas (1989, 1992) goes beyond the state-economism of Keohane and many others (note, Amadae 2015 traces the causes of the decline of virtues and common good in the American political system to the economism of rational choice theory, notably the game theory Prisoner's

Dilemma model[10]). Haas argues that transnational expert communities, who share epistemic standpoints, take part in state, regional and global level interest and identity formation, often facilitating cooperation. Rules and institutional arrangements are important, because they enable and facilitate learning that can lead to the convergence of state policies. For example, Ikenberry suggests that the origin of Bretton Woods should not be seen merely in terms of US structural power but also an epistemic community of British and US economists and policy specialists, which fostered the Anglo-American agreement (Ikenberry 1992).

The concept of epistemic community is similar to the world order model, but more limited. For Braithwaite and Drahos (2000), the world has been post-hegemonic for some time in the sense that under certain circumstances the will and initiatives of many other states and NGOs and key individuals beyond the US have made a difference. Moreover, the role of transnational networks and epistemic communities has often been decisive. Since Braithwaite and Drahos's book, the role of the BRICS has grown, as the stalemate of the WTO Doha round indicates.

The neo-Gramscians have gone further toward developing a dialectical account of the development of global institutions of cooperation. Cox (1987, 1996) emphasized that there are always different social forces involving capabilities for production or destruction; institutional arrangements; and collective understandings. Once created, institutional arrangements "take on their own life" and can "become a battleground for opposing tendencies, or rival institutions may reflect different tendencies". New forms of social existence can emerge, made possible by (new) forms of production but also as a response to the consequences of certain modes and relations of production. Novel forms of social existence necessarily imply new collective understandings and systems of knowledge that are constitutive of their existence and often articulated by organic intellectuals.

Consequently, these emergent new actors, groups and collectives can then contest institutional arrangements, including those that govern the global political economy. Systems are open, change is ubiquitous and everything is historical, although there are patterned processes that enable us to anticipate aspects of the future.[11] The dialectics of world orders occur within existing practical and institutional settings, but may contribute to the transformation of these arrangements and settings.

Trumponomics: its possible and likely global consequences

The demise of Bretton Woods in the early 1970s was a consequence of US unilateral abandonment of dollar–gold convertibility. Contrary to mythologized accounts of "benevolent" US hegemony, the actual historical record reveals contradictory policies by the dominant power throughout the post-Bretton Woods era. The present Trump administration's economic and strategic policies represent important continuities and indeed escalation of past US non-cooperation internationally, rather than an abrupt about-face. Trump's economic and security policies mostly just deepen existing US foreign policy practices, although this may also involve qualitative changes, for example in US trade policy, where self-regard now takes protectionist forms.

Former Chief White House strategist Steve Bannon, in a 2014 speech, invoked the Italian fascist thinker Julius Evola, saying that "changing the system is not a question of questioning and polemicizing, but of blowing everything up" (Navidi 2017). This point of view also reflects a new attitude of greater US assertiveness in foreign and security policy. According to former US Secretary of State Madeleine Albright, attending the Munich security conference in mid-February 2017, representatives from several countries, including Turkey, Iran, China and Russia, made speeches invoking the theme of a post-Western World (Glasser 2017). Albright's impression of reactions from other states to the new US foreign policy stance reveals a change of mood: "there was a sense that the bullying approach of the Trump administration was alienating people rather than giving them solace in terms of the fact that we still were a united world". She lamented that at Munich, the US had moved from being the "centre of attention" to becoming "the centre of doubt" (Glasser 2017).

Alongside a major infrastructure investment plan, the Trump administration aims to execute one of the greatest military build-ups (as upgrades) in American history. The 2018 federal budget outline by the White House also includes a core emphasis on strengthening the US intelligence and national security apparatus, including homeland security and the law enforcement agencies. However, the commitment by the new administration to a balanced budget approach despite the anticipated large increase in military and security expenditure means that many other areas of federal spending must (which is also ideologically desired) involve public–private initiatives and major cuts. A further aim is to reduce cumulatively some ten trillion US dollars in federal spending over a ten-year period.

However, congressional approval and formal appropriation legislation is necessary for these policy ideas to be translated into reality, and this, given the recent history of deep divisions on fiscal policy issues across the political spectrum in Congress, may be doubtful. If the Trump administration's policies are executed in full, they would represent nothing less than a transformation of the state itself, and a reorientation of its primary roles in both domestic and global contexts.

All this is an example of a process that has become self-reinforcing. Pathological learning has reduced collective learning capacity and hardened the will of US foreign policy makers. Trump's election is a further step in this process. Even in the 1990s and early 2000s, there were many cases of international non-cooperation by the US, including ILO conventions, the Law of the Sea Convention, the Convention on Biological Diversity, the Kyoto protocol, the International Criminal Court and the Landmines treaty. The new US administration has now decided to withdraw from the Paris Agreement on climate change, arguably the single most important global issue for effective international cooperation.

The Trump administration's 2018 budget seeks unspecified reductions to US funding for the UN regular and peacekeeping budgets, as part of a 28% reduction in funding for the State Department and US Agency for International Development. Trump's administration has also threatened to withdraw from the UN Human Rights Council, in part due to alleged bias against Israel in that organization.[12] Soros (2002, 166) named the US as "the major obstacle to international cooperation today" as much as 15 years ago. Moreover, Soros shared the observation of many that despite the US holding special responsibility due to its globally dominant position, the US has "not always sought to abide by the same rules that apply to others" (167).

US double standards in its external relations (paralleling similar internal practices, originating in corporate power), and the dogged pursuit of its own national sovereignty and narrow national interests, contradicts and undermines the course of international cooperation and thus destabilizes the world economy. The irony in this historical situation is that the US appears, both past and present, to assume that despite its own actions others will nevertheless continue to abide by the agreed rules, norms and principles. Future scenarios of global change now largely pivot upon how others respond to changes in US attitudes and actions. A spiral of aggressive actions and retaliatory reactions could be set in motion. The probable long-term consequences of such a pattern are quite well known, as any reading of the first half of the twentieth century, and especially the 1930s, reveals (Moser 2016).

There are 2 x 3 different possibilities, some of them more likely than others, as depicted in Table 4.1. First, there are two possibilities regarding how radical

Table 4.1 Six scenarios about the effects of Trumponomics, especially in trade

	Double standards (no retaliation by others)	*Limited retaliation targeted to the US*	*Generalized "beggar-thy-neighbour" policies*
Moderate Trump	A	B	
Radical Trump		C	D

Trump's foreign economic and security policies will turn out. It is possible, in principle, that because of checks and balances and multiple interests within the US, and by learning from experience about the effects of decentralized tit-for-tat sanctions brought about by the international systems of cooperation, Trump will eventually moderate his stance on at least some issues.

The full realization of the stated aims of the Trump administration may require increasingly overt authoritarianism, which in turn is likely to lead to widespread resistance within the US, including presidential impeachment. This scenario entails intensifying domestic conflict and ideological polarization, already arguably rather severe. Such conflict, including in potentially violent forms, could precipitate calls to restore order, thus reinforcing the trend towards erosion of checks and balances and greater domestic repression of the opposition. However unlikely it may still be, a civil war in the US is no longer an excluded possibility.

Out of the six possibilities, four seem relevant in practice. Moderate Trump is compatible with (A) double standards or (B) limited retaliation. Radical Trump will either (C) trigger limited and targeted retaliation against the US (the rest of the world will continue to abide by the rules of the WTO and bilateral and regional free trade arrangements amongst themselves) or (D) create a generalizable example to be followed, leading to widespread "beggar-thy-neighbour" policies. B and C mean that US share of world imports (already down from 17% 2000 to just 12% 2013) and US share of world exports (already down from 12% 2000 to just above 8% 2013) will likely fall further.[13] D would provoke, at minimum, global recession and, at maximum, severe global depression.

The Trump administration has already announced a new foreign trade doctrine, known officially as the "America First Trade Policy".[14] The United States Trade Representative website describes the aims of this policy as "ensuring that American workers are given a fair shot at competing across the globe . . . On a level playing field, Americans can compete fairly and win." It is a central policy goal to keep existing companies located within the US and that overall "companies compete to set up manufacturing in the US", thus generating new jobs, tax revenues and prosperity.

However, as argued above, the majority of jobs recently lost in the US economy seem to be due to automation more than to the effects of foreign trade or off-shoring. The degree to which this new US trade doctrine of America First will be neo-mercantilist in orientation remains to be seen, but the president has previously indicated that the US could potentially impose unilateral trade tariffs on partners that in its view are not playing fair with the US. This includes signatories to past and future trade agreements with the US who subsequently, in US perception, do not correctly fulfil their obligations under the agreement.

According to the president, the US could cancel any trade agreement after a 30-day grace period during which the US would seek compliance by their trade partner. During his first few days in office, President Trump used executive powers to order US withdrawal from the Transpacific Trade Partnership agreement (TTP), to the consternation of several key trade partners, including Japan and Australia, who have been supporting the multilateral agreement. In July 2017, it remains unclear what will happen to the TTIP (Transatlantic Trade and Investment Partnership). The Trade in Services Agreement (TiSA) seems more in line with the ideology of the Trump administration than the TTP or TTIP, and it appears that the US continues to participate in the TiSA negotiations. These negotiations basically concern deregulation (or neoliberal re-regulation) and privatization.

Trade protectionism via tariffs or complicated tax arrangements are not the only form of potential beggar-thy-neighbour policies. Attempts to enhance external competitiveness by means of internal devaluation or tax competition can be equally harmful, albeit in a different way. Many countries, and the EU, have been keen to increase their competitiveness in this sense. The idea is to increase demand for national goods and services in the world markets – at the expense of other countries. World imports and exports cancel out. Although it is not impossible for all countries to simultaneously increase the value of their exports and imports, their overall sum is always zero. The same holds true for investments.

Similarly, if corporate tax cuts have a positive effect on the level of real investments in one given country, it will likely do so at the expense of other countries. This is because there is no aggregate level historical evidence that corporate tax cuts would increase the overall pool of investments. Rather the opposite seems to be true: investment rates have been declining, at least in the OECD world (if not in expanding economies such as China and India). Combined with measures of austerity (that may appear desirable to budget-balancers in part because of the budgetary effects of the tax cuts), these kinds of downward spirals tend to reduce total efficient demand regionally and, to a degree, globally. Overt protectionism would come on top of these other measures and strengthen their already significant effects.

The Trump administration also proposes financial deregulation and tax cuts for corporations and the richest 1% of income earners (one estimate predicts that under Trump's tax reform measures, the top 1% of income earners would see their annual income increase by 13.5%, while average earners' incomes would increase by only 1.8% (Navidi 2017). Financial deregulation would annul the (limited) corrective measures and learning concerning re-regulation of the financial sector (Mackintosh 2016) that followed the global financial crisis. US financial deregulation enacted now may have the further effect of impeding future global cooperation in this area. On 2 February 2017, President Trump, by executive order, demanded a review of the Dodd-Frank Act, whose remit was to prevent/manage/contain future crises. Trump's review resonates with TiSA financial deregulation aims.

The stated aim of the new round of deregulation is to make US financial companies more competitive, but likely at the expense of global financial stability. The periodic crises since the late 1970s have been part of a larger boom–bust process. The underlying super-bubble based on credit expansion and financial multiplication has grown in potential for three decades. It has continued to grow after the weak recovery from the global crisis of 2008–2009; and it has been gradually assembling conditions for an even bigger crash probably in the late 2010s, at the latest in the early 2020s (Patomäki 2010, 79–80). The Trump administration's financial deregulation policy seems to make an early large-scale financial bust more likely. The effects of financial deregulation, combined with other aspects affecting the future stability of respect for the rule of law within the US, may also have the unintended consequence of decreasing the attractiveness of the US as a global economic "safe-haven".

Tax cuts for the rich may also be accompanied by lax policy toward global tax havens facilitating avoidance, although economic nationalism logically encourages an interest in collection of US corporations' worldwide profits. Financialization and the growing financial super-bubble contribute to growing inequalities by increasing r and decreasing g in Piketty's r > g (without fully endorsing his concepts or analysis; see Chapter 5). Growing inequalities have added to the volume of speculation because the rich tend to consume only a small part of their extra income. For the same reason, tax cuts to the rich also have the lowest fiscal multiplier and weakest stimulating effect on the economy, thus probably aggravating the US federal budget deficit. The Fed can of course print more money, but not limitlessly and without consequences.

In terms of trade policy, only (D) in Table 4.1 would take the world *directly* to a situation reminiscent of the early 1930s, while B and C are also a step in the same direction. Moreover, there is another path that may lead to the same outcome as (D). A new major global financial crash during Trump's first term could easily trigger a further worldwide round of growing economic nationalism. It is worth stressing that in 2007–2008 it was the relatively benign international political context that prevented the bad situation from getting worse (Kishner 2014, 47). Disintegration means that next time the international political environment will be less benign.

Conclusions: disabling effects and the possibility of transformative praxes

The current US course seems likely to create conditions for a new era of international discord, leading to further destabilization of the neoliberal world order model that it had itself co-designed (to project and protect its own advantages, interests and values on a world scale). Of course, Trump is erratic; and whether and to what extent Trump's proposals will attain full Congressional approval and legislative authorization remains open, given the fiscal conservatism of many Republicans, and scepticism and resistance amongst many Democrats in Congress. The debacles concerning healthcare and Russia connections are a part of these struggles.

Path-dependent unintended effects of on-going developments in the US and many other parts of the world are producing the next major crisis, possibly stirring up a process that leads to a major catastrophe. These unintended consequences will be disabling, calling into question the prevailing world order model, including its characteristic modes of subjectivity, practices and institutions.

Largely as a consequence of Trump, there has emerged "a lack of consensus even on what a liberal order is" (Leonard 2017). There is growing perception and global comment that the era of Western liberal dominance is ending, and that a post-Western world order is dawning. At the same time, a Polanyian double movement is in motion, with right ideological manifestations being dominant for the time being. However, the whole idea of a world order is once again contested. The historical outcome of this global contestation, both ideologically and practically, will turn upon how states and social forces around the world act and respond in the coming period of global history. This outcome is indeterminate. Reality involves complex multi-path developmental processes that can be interwoven, or contradictory. These overall processes are the topic of the rest of the book.

It would be premature to conclude that because historical developments are not smooth and linear, and because many developments at present seem regressive or chaotic, that there is no rational and progressive direction to world history. We can anticipate the construction of new common institutions of international cooperation and global governance or government; evolving, in evolutionary or dialectical fashion, replacing certain aspects of the authority of territorial sovereign states with more adequate (social, Keynesian, democratic) regional and global arrangements. They can be anticipated in terms of overcoming definite lacks, absences, problems and contradictions of the world economy incrementally or through many simultaneous institutional transformations. The main problem lies in addressing the concerns of people's everyday life.

Notes

1 Peebles (2017) provides an alarmist account (cf. WHO 2016). One problem with the data is that modern psychology and psychiatry take part in constructing new categories of illnesses and disorders, and there is a tendency to medicalize mental and social-psychological phenomena. It is thus not clear what effects are independent of the shifting cultural meanings and power/knowledge regimes of modern capitalist market society (see Foucault 2008).
2 See the numerous commentaries by intellectual and political elites, distributed by Project Syndicate, e.g. Fischer (2017) and Leonard (2017).
3 US income distribution and economic inequality have been widely documented and analysed; see Rasmus (2010, E70–4, 215–23); Mah-Hui and Khor (2011); and Wisman and Baker (2011).
4 See e.g. Erik Sherman, "What a Trump Administration Might Mean for Income Inequality." *Forbes*, November 12, 2016. www.forbes.com/sites/eriksherman/2016/11/12/what-a-trump-administration-might-mean-for-income-inequality/#5cff77d23a78; Gina Chon, "American Inequality Will Widen under Trump in 2017." *Reuters*, December 29, 2016. www.reuters.com/article/us-usa-trump-breakingviews-idUSKBN14I1II; Charles Ballard, "Many of Trump's Policies Will Further Intensify Income Inequality." *The Hill*, February 10, 2017. http://thehill.com/blogs/pundits-blog/economy-budget/318941-many-of-trumps-policies-will-further-intensify-income.
5 The explanation also resonates with Habermas's (1987) thesis concerning the colonization of the lifeworld by the instrumentalist systems of money (capitalist markets) and power (bureaucratic state). The quantified media of money and power that may follow a Kafkaesque or Marxian logic tend to destroy meanings and genuine communication, while remaining dependent on them.
6 Note, Kindleberger fails to account for neo-imperialism 1874–1914 (see Patomäki 2008).
7 It is worth noting that Gilpin's and Kindleberger's list is similar to what Bull (1977) identifies as constitutive of "order", which in turn is exactly the same as Hume's principles of justice in capitalist market society. The three fundamental rules of Humean justice, namely, stability of possession, transfer by consent and keeping of promises, are claimed to be "laws of nature".
8 Grunberg (1990) argues that the appeal of the theory stems from its mythic structure. The day-to-day dilemmas of US foreign policy makers are mixed with American ethnocentrism, assumptions about the benevolence of the US and claims that the "small exploit the rich" (this claim is at the heart of neoliberal discourse, discussed in Chapter 2). Further, the theory uncritically accepts the idea that free trade and security of property rights are public goods.
9 According to Triffin (1961, see also 1968), if the US stopped running balance of payments deficits, the world economy would lose its largest source of additions to reserves. The resulting shortage of liquidity could pull the world economy into a contractionary spiral. If US deficits continued, a steady stream of dollars would continue to stimulate world economic growth. However, US deficits erode confidence in the value of dollar, affecting its status as the world's reserve currency. The fixed exchange rate system could break down, leading to instability. Triffin's idea was to create new reserve units. These units would not depend on gold or currencies, but would add to the world's total liquidity. Creating such

a new reserve would allow the US to reduce its balance of payments deficits, while still allowing for global economic expansion.
10 Among other uses, game theory was applied to develop nuclear strategies for the US during the Cold War. It is best seen as *constitutive* of some key state practices rather than as an external explanation of them.
11 In the early 1990s, Cox (1996, 231–2, 311) foresaw remarkably well likely developments of the next 25 years. He analysed the neoliberal era in terms of a global Polanyian double movement and contestations among different social forces and world order models. The decline of hegemony in the system "undermines conviction in the legitimacy of the principles upon which the globalization thrust is grounded". Segmented polarization leads to identity politics, where nationalism rises and "Islam, for instance can become a metaphor for Third World revolt against Western capitalist domination". "The other tendency is toward a world of economic blocs", competing for shares in world markets and raw materials. And "a financial crisis is the most likely way in which the existing world order could begin to collapse".
12 "Rex Tillerson Threatens to Withdraw from UN Human Rights Council to Improve Human Rights Secretary of State Is Deciding Where and How to Cut $10 Billion of US Funding to the UN", *The Independent*, Wednesday March 15, 2017. www.independent.co.uk/news/world/americas/rex-tillerson-un-human-rights-council-us-secretary-state-china-saudi-arabia-egypt-a7630531.html.
13 Export and import data suggests a rapid decline in US competitiveness, but reality is more complicated. For example, Mandel (2012) argues that the decline is mostly due to the changing composition of the products traded internationally (the rest of the world is increasingly trading goods that the US does not produce) and the diminished share of US GDP in global output, i.e. not due to the relative competitiveness of US firms.
14 See United States Trade Representative: https://ustr.gov/.

References

Alker, Hayward, Tahir Amin, Thomas Biersteker, and Takashi Inoguchi. 1996. "Concluding Reflections on the Dialectics of World Order." Paper prepared for the ISA-JAIR Joint Convention, Makuhari Prince Hotel, Japan, September 20–22. http://dornsife.usc.edu/assets/sites/556/docs/concluding_reflections.PDF.
Amadae, Sonja. 2015. *Prisoners of Reason: Game Theory and Neoliberal Political Economy*. Cambridge: Cambridge University Press.
APSA (The American Political Science Association). 2004. "American Democracy in an Age of Rising Inequality." *Task Force on Inequality and American Democracy*, July 26. www.apsanet.org/Inequality/taskforcereport.pdf.
Axelrod, Robert. 1984. *The Evolution of Cooperation*. New York: Basic Books.
Braithwaite, John, and Peter Drahos. 2000. *Global Business Regulation*. Cambridge: Cambridge University Press.
Bull, Hedley. 1977. *The Anarchical Society: A Study of Order in World Politics*. Houndmills, Basingstoke: MacMillan.
Chernomas, Robert, and Ian Hudson. 2017. *The Profit Doctrine: Economists of the Neoliberal Era*. London: Pluto Press.

Cox, Robert. 1987. *Production, Power and World Order: Social Forces in the Making of History*. New York: Columbia University Press.
Cox, Robert. 1996. *Approaches to World Order*. Cambridge: Cambridge University Press.
Der Spiegel. 2017. "Donald Trump and the New World Order." *Der Spiegel*, January 20. www.spiegel.de/international/world/trump-inauguration-signals-new-world-order-a-1130916.html.
Fischer, Joschka. 2017. "Turning towards Authoritarianism: Is Trump Taking the US Down Turkey's Path?" *Project Syndicate, Posted on Euronews.com*, February 27. www.euronews.com/2017/02/27/view-turning-towards-authoritarianism-is-trump-taking-the-us-down-turkeys-path.
Foucault, Michel. 2008. *Mental Illness and Psychology*. 2nd revised ed. Berkeley: University of California Press.
Gilpin, Robert. 1981. *War and Change in World Politics*. Cambridge: Cambridge University Press.
Gilpin, Robert. 1987. *The Political Economy of International Relations*. Princeton: Princeton University Press.
Glasser, Susan. 2017. "The Alpha Males Are Back." *Politico Magazine*, February 27.
Grunberg, Isabelle. 1990. "Exploring the 'Myth' of Hegemonic Stability." *International Organization* 44 (4): 431–77.
Haas, Peter. 1989. "Do Regimes Matter? Epistemic Communities and Mediterranean Pollution Control." *International Organization* 43 (3): 377–403.
Haas, Peter. 1992. "Introduction: Epistemic Communities and International Policy Coordination." *International Organization* 46 (1): 1–35.
Habermas, Jürgen. 1987. *The Theory of Communicative Action*. Vol. 2. Translated by Thomas McCarthy. Boston: Beacon Press.
Harvey, David. 2005. *A Brief History of Neoliberalism*. Oxford: Oxford University Press.
Ikenberry, John. 1992. "A World Economy Restored: Expert Consensus and the Anglo-American Postwar Settlement." *International Organization* 46 (1): 289–321.
Keohane, Robert. 1980. "The Theory of Hegemonic Stability and Changes in International Economic Regimes, 1967–77." In *Change in the International System*, edited by Ole R. Holsti, Randolph M. Siverson, and Alexander L. George, 131–62. Boulder, CO: Westview Press.
Keohane, Robert. 2005. *After Hegemony: Cooperation and Discord in the World Political Economy*. Princeton Classic Edition, with a New Preface. Princeton: Princeton University Press.
Kindleberger, Charles. 1973. *The World in Depression 1929–1939*. London: Allen Lane Penguin Press.
Kindleberger, Charles. 1981. "Dominance and Leadership in the International Economy: Exploitation, Public Goods and Free Riders." *International Studies Quarterly* 25 (2): 242–54.
Kishner, Jonathan. 2014. "International Relations Then and Now: Why the Great Recession Was Not the Great Depression." *History of Economic Ideas* 22 (3): 47–69.

Krasner, Stephen. 1976. "State Power and the Structure of International Trade." *World Politics* 28 (3): 317–47.

Layne, Christopher. 2012. "This Time It's Real: The End of Unipolarity and the Pax Americana." *International Studies Quarterly* 56 (1): 203–13.

Leonard, Mark. 2017. "Will the Liberal Order Survive? If So, Which Version?" *Project Syndicate, Posted on Euronews.com*, February 28. www.euronews.com/2017/02/28/view-will-the-liberal-order-survive-if-so-which-version.

Mackintosh, Stuart P. M. 2016. *The Redesign of the Global Financial Architecture: The Return of State Authority*. London: Routledge.

Mah-Hui, Michael Lim, and Khor Hoe Ee. 2011. "From Marx to Morgan Stanley: Inequality and Financial Crisis." *Development and Change* 42: 209–27. doi: 10.1111/j.1467-7660.2011.01693.x.

Mandel, Benjamin R. 2012. "Why Is the U.S. Share of World Merchandise Exports Shrinking?" *Current Issues, Federal Reserve Bank of New York* 18 (1). www.newyorkfed.org/research/current_issues.

Mayhew, Anne. 2017. "Trump through a Polanyi Lens: Considering Community Well-Being." *Real-World Economics Review* (78): 28–35.

Moser, John E. 2016. *The Global Great Depression and the Coming of World War II*. London: Routledge.

Navidi, Sandra. 2017. "American Democracy: Will Trump Blow Everything Up?" *Project Syndicate 2017, Posted on Euronews*, February 28.

Palast, Greg. 2004. *The Best Democracy Money Can Buy: An Investigative Reporter Exposes the Truth about Globalization, Corporate Cons and High Finance Fraudsters*. New York: Plume (Penguin).

Patomäki, Heikki. 2008. *The Political Economy of Global Security: War, Future Crises and Changes in Global Governance*. London: Routledge.

Patomäki, Heikki. 2010. "What Next? An Explanation of the 2008–2009 Slump and Two Scenarios for the Shape of Things to Come." *Globalizations* 7 (1): 67–84.

Peebles, Graham. 2017. "The Rise of Anxiety in the Age of Inequality." *Open Democracy*, May 20. www.opendemocracy.net/graham-peebles/anxiety-in-age-of-inequality?utm_source=Daily+Newsletter&utm_campaign=b74a3edfa1-DAILY_NEWSLETTER_MAILCHIMP&utm_medium=email&utm_term=0_717bc5d86d-b74a3edfa1-407375311.

Pettifor, Ann. 2017. "Causes and Consequences of President Donald Trump." *Real-World Economics Review* (78): 44–53. www.paecon.net/PAEReview/issue78/Pettifor78.pdf.

Pickett, Kate, and Richard Wilkinson. 2010. *The Spirit Level: Why Equality Is Better for Everyone*. New York: Bloomsbury Press.

Putnam, Robert D. 2001. *Bowling Alone: The Collapse and Revival of American Community*. New York: Simon & Schuster.

Rasmus, Jack. 2010. *Epic Recession: Prelude to Global Depression*. London: Pluto Press.

Richards, Lindsay, and Marii Paskov. 2016. "Social Class, Employment Status and Inequality in Psychological Well-Being in the UK: Cross-Sectional and Fixed Effects Analyses over Two Decades." *Social Science & Medicine* 167: 45–53.

Rodrik, Dani. 2001. *The Global Governance of Trade as If Development Really Mattered*. Revised July 2001. Cambridge, MA: John F. Kennedy School of Government. www.giszpenc.com/globalciv/rodrik1.pdf.

Ruggie, John G. 1982. "International Regimes, Transactions, and Change: Embedded Liberalism in the Postwar Economic Order." *International Organization* 36 (2): 379–415.

Saez, Emmanuel. 2016. "Striking It Richer: The Evolution of Top Incomes in the United States. Summary for the Broader Public." University of California at Berkeley. http://eml.berkeley.edu/~saez/saez-UStopincomes-2015.pdf.

Soros, George. 2002. *On Globalization*. New York: PublicAffairs.

Springer, Simon, Kean Birch, and Julie MacLeavy, eds. 2016. *The Handbook of Neoliberalism*. London: Routledge.

Steger, Manfred. 2009. *Globalisms: The Great Ideological Struggle of the Twenty-First Century*. 3rd ed. Lanham, MD: Rowman & Littlefield.

Stiglitz, Joseph E. 2003. *The Roaring Nineties: A New History of the World's Most Prosperous Decade*. New York: W.W. Norton.

Stiglitz, Joseph E. 2013. *The Price of Inequality*. London: Penguin Books.

Strange, Susan. 1987. "The Persistent Myth of Lost Hegemony." *International Organization* 41 (4): 551–74.

Triffin, Robert. 1961. *Gold and the Dollar Crisis*. New Haven: Yale University Press.

Triffin, Robert. 1968. *Our International Monetary System: Yesterday, Today, and Tomorrow*. New York: Random House.

Unger, Roberto Mangabeira. 2007. *Free Trade Reimagined: The World Division of Labor and the Method of Economics*. Princeton: Princeton University Press.

WHO (World Health Organisation). 2016. *Investing in Treatment for Depression and Anxiety Leads to Fourfold Return*. Joint News Release WHO & World Bank, April 13. www.who.int/mediacentre/news/releases/2016/depression-anxiety-treatment/en/.

Wisman, Jon D., and Barton Baker. 2011. "Increasing Inequality, Inadequate Demand, Status Insecurity, Ideology, and the Financial Crises of 2008." Working Paper No. 1–12–11, American University. www.american.edu/cas/economics/pdf/upload/2011-1.pdf.

Wohlforth, William C. 2012. "How Not to Evaluate Theories." *International Studies Quarterly* 56 (1): 219–22.

Wolin, Sheldon. 2010. *Democracy Incorporated: Managed Democracy and the Specter of Inverted Totalitarianism*. Princeton: Princeton University Press.

Young, Oran. 1989. "The Politics of International Regime Formation: Managing Natural Resources and the Environment." *International Organization* 43 (3): 349–75.

Young, Oran. 1991. "Political Leadership and Regime Formation: On the Development of Institutions in International Society." *International Organization* 45 (3): 281–308.

5 Piketty's inequality r > g

The key to understanding and overcoming the dynamics of disintegration

The word integration comes from the Latin *integratus*, past participle of *integrare*, meaning "to make whole". In French and English, the meaning of integration as "to put together parts or elements and combine them into a whole" has been common for centuries. Its antonyms include disunion, division, separation and divorce. Brexit is an example of separation; the conflict in Ukraine stems from divisions and discords that also concern Russia and the EU; and Trump's economic and other policies tend to heighten regional borders and create major global rifts. These and other disintegrative developments in global political economy have involved slowdowns of economic growth, sudden economic crises and growing inequalities.

One of the key claims of Piketty's *Capital in the Twenty-First Century* (2014) is that there is a tendency for $r > g$, where r is the average annual rate of return on capital and g is annual economic growth. This is especially likely for regimes of slow growth. When this simple inequality holds it means that past wealth is becoming more important and inherited wealth grows faster than output and income.[1] If this is combined with the inequality of returns on financial or other investments as a function of initial wealth, the result is an increasing concentration of wealth and capital (443). For Piketty, this is the "fundamental inequality" of capitalist market society, closely connected to its two "fundamental laws". My question in this chapter is: Is the expression $r > g$ also a key to understanding the dynamics of disintegration in the world economy, especially as deceleration of growth and mounting inequalities also have implications on democracy and processes of political legitimation?

Piketty's claim that $r > g$ has been subject to much criticism (for a systematic review, see King 2017). The average annual rate of return on capital, r, conflates wealth (almost any asset with market value) and capital, K, that is actually used in the production process. A key part of capital in this sense K is human skills and know-how (e.g. Knibbe 2014, 159–61). Piketty relies on a number of standard ideas of neoclassical economics and thus ends up assuming, by default more than on purpose, and not always consistently, that involuntary unemployment cannot prevail, that labour has no bargaining power and that investments are not influenced by overall demand in the economy (Varoufakis 2014). Moreover, Piketty's account is also too deterministic, often verging on the tautological. His equations lack Keynesian endogeneity and over-simplify the consumption relation of wealth and income. They do not make it possible to calculate r for most historical periods (Mihalyi and Szelényi 2016). In open systems, technological changes and innovations – for instance in credit creation – can affect rates of return on different types of investments. Equally importantly, wealth and income distribution depend on institutional arrangements and power relations, as Piketty at times acknowledges. In contrast to neoclassical models, on which Piketty relies in many parts of his argument, they "have relatively little to do with marginal productivity in complete and profit-maximizing competitive market-models" (Syll 2014, 69). Last but not least, also Piketty's datasets and data-representations have been argued to be unreliable (Galbraith and Halbach 2016; Wright 2015).

I am in broad agreement with most of these critiques. I take Piketty's simple expression $r > g$ not as "fundamental" or as a "law", but as an organizing scheme with which we can explore the possible and likely consequences of g getting smaller; and something akin to Piketty's r getting larger. For a quarter of a century r was smaller than g, but since about 1980, $r > g$ has held, and this change captures and summarizes many of those complex open-systemic processes that have resulted in the current disintegrative tendencies in global political economy. Piketty is right in thinking that r and g are related. The rate of per capita growth of the world economy first declined in the 1970s, when the Bretton Woods system in its original form came to an end, and then further in the early 1980s, with the advent of the global debt problem and the ascendance of neoliberalism. In Japan, Europe and North America, the decline of growth rates has continued unabated until the late 2010s.

As documented also by Piketty (2014, 22–7), both income inequalities and the wealth/income ratio started to rise in the 1970s and 1980s. This type of process easily becomes self-reinforcing via changing relations of power. Progressively more uneven power relations have meant that the wealthiest 1% especially, but also the wealthiest 10% or 20%, have tended to increase their share of incomes and wealth. Income inequalities are only a part of the story. Asset price inflation in crisis-prone housing markets and, most importantly, in the volatile global financial markets have enabled the rich to translate their higher propensity to save to be translated into a constantly increasing share of aggregate wealth (cf. Varoufakis 2014, 52; see Patomäki 2001, ch 2). A dramatic illustration of the power of these mechanisms and tendencies is that by Oxfam's (2017) estimate, by 2016 eight men have come to own the same wealth as the 3.6 billion people who make up the poorest half of humanity.

In the first section of this chapter, I describe and briefly analyse how growth rates and socio-economic inequalities are related. The difference between r and g has been growing, because GDP growth has slowed and because financialization and related deflationary consequences have in effect increased r. There are many possible explanations for this dynamic. Natural limits to growth may have started to bite. Deindustrialization and the changing composition of the economy have diminished GDP growth potential, especially in high-income countries; but I argue that the deceleration of growth is due mainly to economic policy and cumulative causation related to the geo-economic shifts of uneven growth. Economic policy in turn is determined by relations of power.

Like many other researchers of inequalities, Piketty maintains that the developments we are now observing are likely to erode democracy and are difficult to reverse. So far only major catastrophes and especially two world wars have constituted sufficiently powerful shocks to change the direction of what he considers "fundamental" or "law-like" developments. Upon closer inspection, reality is more complicated. Reversing Piketty's problematic, however, I argue that the concentration of wealth and the rising importance of past and inherited wealth are making a major economic and political disaster more likely under current conditions.

I conclude that the expression $r > g$ captures some of the essential dynamics of the disintegrative tendencies in the global political economy. It follows that Piketty is also normatively right: something must be done. Piketty (2014, 532) argues that new solutions that a global tax on capital is the most appropriate response to this tendency towards socio-economic divergence and disparities. He considers it a utopian idea, but possibly realizable on a regional basis, perhaps even in the relatively short run. The proposal for a global tax on wealth plays a critical role in Piketty's overall argument. It is the chief normative conclusion from his analysis of the causes of the concentration of wealth.

I concur with Piketty that new tools are required to regain democratic control over the globalized financial capitalism, and that a global tax on capital is a promising idea. Toward the end of this chapter, I make further three points. First, tax reforms are not only made possible or at least easier by major wars, as Piketty maintains; arguably it is also true that concentration of wealth makes major wars more likely. This point strengthens Piketty's argument and underlines the urgency of reform.

Second, on a more critical note, the choice between a utopian global approach and a more feasible regional approach to the tax is misleading. There are easier ways to realize a global tax. Third, while Piketty's exclusive focus on wealth distribution may make it plausible to assume that a single global tax would suffice to reverse the trends of the past decades, in reality economic policy involves many issues and concerns a number of other processes. A global tax on capital would have to be accompanied by a more general shift towards global Keynesian economic policies. This would not necessarily make changes more difficult.

The slow-down of growth

It is important that we understand the interpretative and metaphorical nature of claims about economic waves and eras. Even quantitative data and its underlying data-coding procedures are theory-laden. For instance, Anwar Shaikh argues in his *magnum opus* that "the history of capitalism over the centuries reveals recurring patterns of long booms and busts" (Shaikh 2016, 726; reviewed Patomäki 2017). In his figure 16.1, Shaikh displays what he calls the "US and UK golden waves", or long waves of national price levels measured in terms of gold. His figure seems to indicate an upward long wave from 1980 to 2007. I disagree. I have previously expressed the opinion that there is no upward turning point in the early 1980s (Patomäki 2008, ch 5). Our differences point to the difficulties of reading macrohistory, that is, of telling plausible stories about world history.

In Shaikh's figure 16.1, he assumes price-level deviations from a fitted cubic trend, where price levels are measured in terms of gold (the price of which varies for all kinds of reasons, not least in response to turbulence in the financial markets). He must then take many steps of theory-laden interpretation to move from this assumption to his conclusion that there was an extended upward long wave in the world economy in 1983–2007. Just as plausibly, this wave may reflect changes in the price of gold, which would be consistent with the hypothesis of rising volatility and uncertainties due to financialization.

As a measure of economic activities and value, GDP is biased in several ways, favouring private market transactions and commodification. GDP is not a measure of welfare or well-being (see note 8 of Chapter 2). Many parts of it are estimated rather than observed directly. GDP comparisons involve many choices, for instance about the base year and measure of value. We can nonetheless use it as the most readily available proxy for economic activity and value produced.

Figures 5.1 and 5.2 display world and high-income countries' GDP per capita growth rates as measured in constant 2010 US dollars during the last half-century. These figures include a dotted line indicating a moving average of the past ten years. In the light of these two figures, the existence of what Shaikh considers an upward long wave from the early 1980s to 2007 is a matter of perspective. In Figure 5.1, if we look at the moving

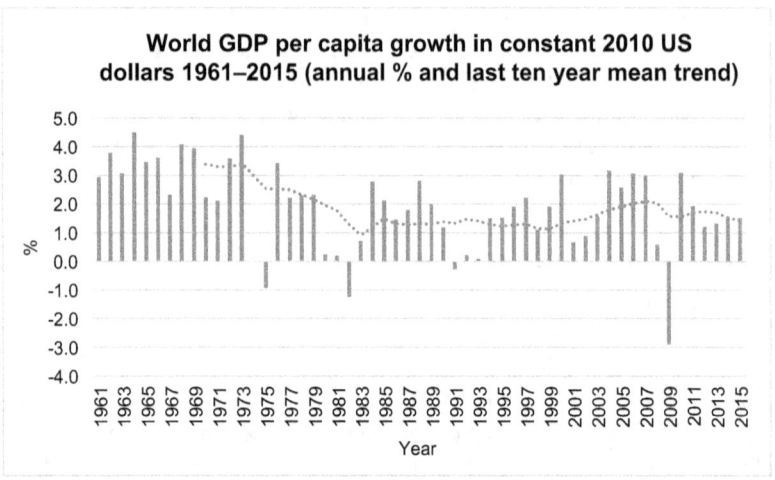

Figure 5.1 World GDP per capita growth rates

Source: Data from World Bank 2017, *World Development Indicators*, at http://databank.worldbank.org/data/reports.aspx?source=2&series=NY.GDP.MKTP.CD&country=WLD#.

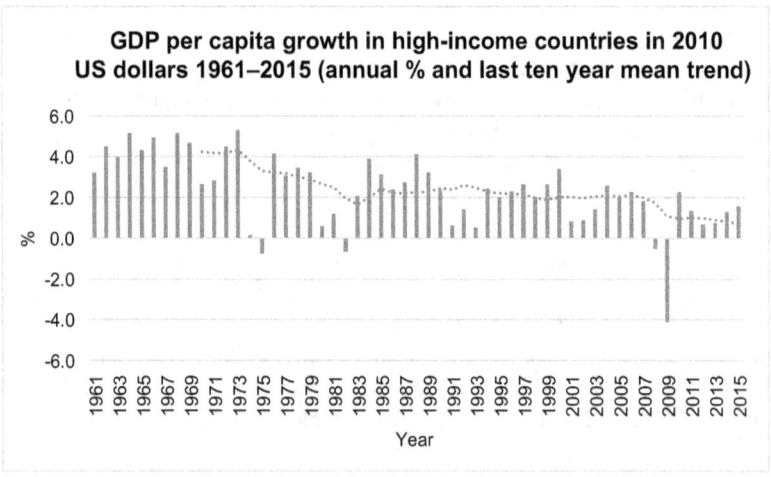

Figure 5.2 High-income countries' GDP per capita growth rates

Source: Data from World Bank 2017, *World Development Indicators*, at http://databank.worldbank.org/data/reports.aspx?source=2&series=NY.GDP.MKTP.CD&country=WLD#.

average and select 1983 as the base year, the period until 2008 was indeed a period of continuing and accelerating growth. However, in the 1960s and 1970s the average growth rates was 3–4% per capita. This was the "golden age of capitalism" and state socialism. These average rates started to decline in the 1970s, reaching 1% in 1983. Since then they have varied between 1% and 2%.

Growth deceleration in high-income countries has been more systematic and persistent, as Figure 5.2 shows. The difference between world and high-income country is mostly due to the growing weight of China and India. In 1992, their share of the world economy was 7.9% and in 2015 24.2%. This is especially significant for the post-2007 trend. For high-income countries, the moving average has fallen below 1%, and we know that for the Eurozone average output growth 2009–2016 was 0.4% (Table 2.2). This is low even when compared to late-nineteenth-century rates.

The starting point for adequate analysis of these trends is that they occur in open systems with many tendencies and mechanisms. Social systems are also overlapping and inter- and intra-related (this is a key reason why we should consider the whole global political economy as our chief unit of analysis). The effects of various tendencies and mechanisms can be delayed, overlapping, mutually reinforcing and/or contradictory. In open systems, what explanation works and what does not work always depends on many things. Simple invariant regularities do not occur and unconditional conclusions are rarely warranted.

One obvious explanation for the slow-down in OECD countries is that the composition of the economy has changed: deindustrialization has been coupled with a growing share of services. In many service sectors, labour productivity does not rise at all, while in others only a little. Orchestral training takes as long today as in the past and almost as many barbers are needed today as before to keep 100 people's hair neat.[2] However, change in the composition of the economy is only part of the economic downturn. Growth has also begun to slow down because of natural limits (limits to nature) to growth, although the effects of these limits are likely to become more apparent only in the 2020s and 2030s.[3]

Arguably, however, the slow-down of economic growth is, especially in high-income countries, a consequence of predominant economic policy. Prevalent economic thinking can have real effects through economic policies and can, in important part, be responsible for the phases of long waves. Keynesian and other heterodox economic theories help to understand the contradictory nature of current economic policy. For instance, the paradox of thrift tells us why the goal of saving by cutting public spending or lowering salaries tends to be counterproductive. This and other economic paradoxes, however, are not just about logic but about the actual behaviour of actors. Their practical realization requires many simultaneous activities to occur in the same direction. Not all actors behave in the same way.[4]

The policies of public authorities have significant effects on the development of the whole economy. Expanding public expenditure will increase total demand, whereas deflationary economic policy reduces overall demand in relation to what would otherwise have been realized (an economy is a process in which all parts are always in motion). An important issue is the magnitude of the multiplier of public expenditure. The higher the multiplier, the more significant the dynamic effects are. Most of the total demand is still domestic. Part of the multiplier effect will flow to other countries, so one important aspect is also what other countries and the EU do and how international organizations and global governance systems work. The multiplier effect is the main reason why austerity does not work.

Differences in demand problems can result in uneven development – long-run growth divergences across countries or regions. This is because processes of uneven growth in the world economy involve not only vicious but virtuous circles of cumulative causation.[5] For instance, the Keynesian demand-led Kaldor-Verdoorn's effect may generate a virtuous circle between output and productivity growth (Kaldor 1966). Claims about the Kaldor-Verdoorn's effect were originally based on an empirical observation that in the long run productivity generally grows proportionally to the square root of output. Output can only grow if there is sufficient demand for the produced goods, so an increase in demand can lead to investments and higher productivity (investments depend on fluctuations of uncertainty that are directly linked to effective total demand; Keynes 1937).

There are two main explanations for the Kaldor-Verdoorn effect: (i) economies of scale prevail in manufacturing and (ii) learning by doing increases skill levels and can lead to innovation. The Kaldor-Verdoorn effect also resonates with the basic idea of new trade theory (Krugman 1979, 1980, 1981). Trade enables markets to grow, increases product diversity, brings benefits from economies of scale and causes real wages to increase. Although a sceptical post-Marxian economist may hold that the subsequent fall in profitability will eventually undermine the effects of increased demand (Shaikh 2016, 654–7), evidently China has sustained this effect continuously since the early 1990s (25 years). A lot hinges on what "eventually" means in real geo-history.

How the slow-down of growth and rising inequalities are intertwined

Prevailing economic policies and corporate practices in the OECD world and elsewhere from the late 1970s and early 1980s has in general increased income and wealth gaps within countries. In some important ways, the same is also true globally, although not in all dimensions (the growing middle classes in China and India implying reverse developments in some dimensions of measurement). The characteristic increase in income inequalities explains in part why GDP growth has declined, because inequality reduces consumer demand, which has multiplier effects.[6] The process of financialization has enabled the rich to translate their higher propensity to save into an increasing share of aggregate wealth, but it has also contributed to a decline in fixed real investment,[7] and at the same time increased instability in the global economy.[8] Moreover, the policies of austerity and competitiveness are contradictory within countries and the global economy, reducing total demand. Countries' simultaneous efforts to increase exports by improving their own price competitiveness confound the goal of economic growth.

The slow-down of growth and rising inequalities are interwoven in complex ways. Arguably they also have a common origin. Korpinen (1981, 14) states an important hypothesis: monetarist, or free-market economic policies, tend to contribute to recession and deflation, and Keynesian and monetarist policies occur in long cycles of learning and unlearning. However, Korpinen does not discuss the role of power relations. The value of money is a key point of political contestation (low inflation benefits those with wealth and liquid capital) and economic policies also involve income distribution. Moreover, power relations based on private property rights and an uneven distribution of property – constitutive of capitalist relations of production and exchange – may in part account for a tendency towards the prevalence of orthodox policy-making. Orthodoxy assumes self-correcting capitalist markets in a state of (approaching) equilibrium that is normally beneficial to all parties.

A key source of the power that has regenerated economic liberal orthodoxy is the discrepancy between the limited reach of territorial states and an open world economy. Neoliberalization originates in conflict over income distribution, competitiveness and power in the context of this widening discrepancy. The power of the neoliberal field stems both from the inner structures of liberal-capitalist market society and from its generic potential for spatial extension (see Harvey 1990, 2005; Patomäki 2008, chs 5–6). Throughout the Bretton Woods era, territorial states remained the main locus of regulation and the sole locus for tax-and-transfer policies. At the same time, the rules and principles of Bretton Woods and GATT were meant to ensure gradual liberalization and re-integration of the world economy.

By the early 1960s, the re-integration of the world economy had presented opportunities for business actors to resolve problems through relocation. The ensuing transformations also involved explicit political choices. President Nixon made the key decision in 1971 to disconnect the value of the US dollar from gold. This was a choice between unilateralism and multilateralism; unilateralism was also justified in terms of a belief in "free markets". The ideas associated with neoliberalism entered the public sphere more forcefully after 1971–1973. Once the structural power of transnational capital and neoliberal globalization had gained the ascendancy, the reinstatement of economic liberalism has followed its own self-reinforcing dynamics (Patomäki 2008, chs 5–6).

The process of reinstating economic liberalism involves positive feedback loops through the realization of its preferred institutional arrangements, which tend to reinforce its potential. The dynamics of this process, characterized by positive feedback to at least some actors, have the power to support and institutionalize the original choice(s). In a reciprocal process, actors may lock themselves into epistemic positions that then constitute their *habitus*, i.e. mode of being and agency. Political settings where one set of actors must initially impose their preferences on another through an open conflict ("the first face of power") may change, rendering open conflict unnecessary because power relations are so skewed that reactions are anticipated (agenda control, "the second face of power") or ideological manipulation arises ("the third face") (cf. Pierson 2004, 37).

In a capitalist market society, the general tendency towards the prevalence of free market policies seems to become stronger when (i) economic developments have been favourable at least in the centres of the world economy, and inflation is increasingly seen as the main problem (see endnote 8); and/or when (ii) the position of private capital becomes more secure in terms of structural power and/or political positioning. Once dominant, however, orthodox policies may contribute to the slowed economic growth through mechanisms efficacious in different geo-historical contexts. Geo-historical differences notwithstanding, there seems to be a general tendency towards gradually deepening deflation, that is, a downward phase involving under-consumption/overproduction, unemployment, stagnating or declining prices, social problems and political reactions. These developments are closely entangled with growing inequalities in incomes and wealth.

Large-scale wars and tax reforms

Although there are no fundamental or unchanging laws in political economy, given the constitutive principles of capitalist market society and the discrepancy between states and the world economy, could it be that only in specific circumstances that countertendencies to orthodoxy become strong enough to make a real difference in policy-making? The twentieth-century world wars were major economic and political shocks. Piketty argues that "we can now see those shocks as the *only* forces since the Industrial Revolution powerful enough to reduce inequality" (2014, 8; italics HP). This is a point repeated several times in *Capital*; he also provides ample statistical evidence on the impact on the level of taxation and inequalities (18–20, 41, 141, 287, 471, 498–500; but for words of caution Galbraith and Halbach 2016; Wright 2015).

Piketty, however, is not fully consistent in formulating this point. Counterfactual developments are uncertain. Without the shock of World War I, "the move toward a more progressive tax system would at the very least have been much slower, and top rates might have never risen as high as they did" (500). The war facilitated and accelerated, but it was not a necessary condition for, change. Democratization too seems to have played a facilitating role: "[P]rogressive taxation was as much a product of two world wars as it was of democracy" (498). One problem is, however, that democracy cannot explain the decline of progressive taxation and the return of widening inequalities since the 1970s.

Piketty turns his world-historical insight – that there is a close relationship between major modern wars and reduced inequalities – into a question about possible futures. Must we wait for the next major (truly global) crisis or war? Or are peaceful and lasting changes possible? (471) For instance, the global financial crisis 2008–2009 was not compelling enough to make any major difference in terms of the underlying structural problems, including the lack of financial transparency (tax havens, etc.) and the rise of inequality. A more devastating economic and political shock seems to be required for real change to become possible.

This is an important problematic. Here I would like to reverse the question. What will the concentration of capital and the rising importance of past and inherited wealth mean to the likelihood of a major economic and political disaster? Piketty maintains that the developments we are now observing are likely to erode democracy. The concentration of capital can become acute – "levels potentially incompatible with the meritocratic values and principles of social justice fundamental to modern democratic societies" (26). Are these high levels also incompatible with democracy *per se*? What are the consequences of de-democratization?

Rawls (1973) states in *A Theory of Justice* that wealth can be translated into political influence in liberal democracies:

> The liberties protected by the principle of participation lose much of their value whenever those who have greater private means are permitted to use their advantages to control the course of public debate. For eventually these inequalities will enable those better situated to exercise a larger influence over the development of legislation. In due time they are likely to acquire a preponderant weight in settling social

questions, at least in regard to those matters upon which they normally agree, which is to say in regard to those things that support their favored circumstances.

(225)

As discussed Chapters 2 and 4, we can clearly observe the effects of such developments in the UK and the US. In the last few decades the US has become especially inegalitarian. For instance, the Task Force on Inequality and American Democracy (APSA 2004), formed under the auspices of the 14,000-member American Political Science Association, concluded "that Progress toward realizing American ideals of democracy may have stalled, and in some arenas reversed". The US political system has become more responsive to the needs and wishes of the privileged than ordinary American citizens. A further problem is that this process is self-reinforcing. Logically, in the absence of powerful countertendencies, over time democracy must become thinner and thinner. Real power relations turn asymmetric, reflecting the hierarchies of the inegalitarian society in which wealth and power are concentrated in the hands of relatively few.

The concentration of wealth shapes the production and distribution of knowledge in society. Humans tend to confirmation bias and filter evidence (Gilovich 1993). This gets stronger in increasingly homogenized organizational contexts (such as funding, ownership and power relations in education and research, media etc). In this process, actors tend to lock themselves in increasingly narrow knowledge/power-positions, constitutive of their ethico-political identity and agency. Anything perceived as threatening basic values may be securitized; and anyone dissenting may be constructed as a potential or actual enemy. The logic of securitization in this sense can boost tendencies towards "inverted totalitarianism" (Wolin 2010).

These developments will not stay at home but spread through international law. New constitutionalism (Gill 1992, 2008) is a political and legal strategy that has been actively pushed by the US and EU to disconnect economic policies from democratic accountability and will-formation by means of international treaties and institutions, often framed in terms of "free trade". Many international treaties and institutions are more difficult to revise than typical national constitutions, providing protection against political changes.

There are two main reasons why these developments increase the likelihood of major economic and political shocks. First, they strengthen the relative power of actors who are predisposed to disregard economic policies needed to ensure full employment and stable economic development. To reiterate points already made, paralleling Kalecki's (1943) argument, business leaders and capitalists wish to create circumstances in which policies depend on their confidence; the scope of free markets is maximized; and hierarchical power relations in the workplace are ensured. Once this is achieved we should expect a slackening growth-trend; and within it unequal growth, concentration of capital and resources, oligopolization or monopolization of world markets and increasing oscillations with perhaps increasing amplitude, not least in finance. Thereby the likelihood of major economic crises and shocks must increase.

Second, de-democratization, securitization, enemy-construction and inverted totalitarianism are liable to generate and aggravate antagonistic relations with different others in a wide range of geo-historical contexts. For instance, the "what is good for us must be good for you" attitude can mean imperial-style involvement in the development of those regions that are either lagging or falling behind or where many actively resist the prevailing or hegemonic direction. Moreover, as Piketty stresses, when countries face increasingly adverse consequences from free market globalization, some also respond by turning to nationalism and forms of protectionism – and to measures which are unacceptable for those who defend free market globalization and its neo-constitutional guarantees. Constellations of forces can change rapidly. When it is the US that turns to nationalism and forms of protectionism, this may become a security issue in the EU. These kinds of juxtapositions can pave the way for conflict escalation, increasing the likelihood of major political shocks, conflicts and war.

Global capital tax: from utopia to a feasible strategy of peaceful changes

If Piketty's general analysis and my causal diagnosis of the prevailing trends pertains, then Brexit, Ukraine and Trump are symptoms of a deeper problem. This problem can also generate great power conflicts. It may, therefore, seem worrying that Piketty presents his global capital tax cure as "utopian". Does this mean that there is no current feasible alternative, that the best we can do is hope that we will survive the inevitable global disaster, and await a subsequent more egalitarian society? What then? Will the cycle continue after this round?

Piketty is far from despairing, although he warns repeatedly of dire consequences of on-going developments:

> Admittedly, a global tax on capital would require a very high and no doubt unrealistic level of international cooperation. But countries wishing to move in this direction could very well do so incrementally, starting with at the regional level (in Europe, for instance). Unless

something like this happens, a defensive reaction of a nationalist stripe would very likely occur.

(515–16)

Optimistically, Piketty praises the recent progress of the proposed financial transaction tax (FTT) in Europe, arguing that "it could become one of the first truly European taxes" (562). Unfortunately, the situation is not simple. In September 2011, the Commission proposed the FTT should be realized in the EU, and is economically necessary and in the interests of fairness. During the global financial crisis, EU leaders also pushed the FTT onto the G20 agenda. At the G20 summit in Cannes November 2011 several countries joined the US in opposing the idea.

The September 2011 Commission proposal comes close to Piketty's idea of "one of the first truly European taxes" (although falling short of the global idealism of the Tobin tax movement). In June 2012, it was concluded that the proposal for a FTT would not be adopted by the Council within a reasonable period, and enhanced cooperation (at last nine member states agree and coordinate to further integration) was the only way to proceed. The UK challenged even this idea in the European Court of Justice. Although the ECJ dismissed the UK's action April 2014, the current proposal seems more like an agreement to jointly implement national taxes than a European tax. Its actual practical form remained undecided summer 2017.

According to Piketty, the FTT is less significant than a tax on capital or corporate profits (562). It is less ambitious than Piketty's proposal, which also confronts problems even if restricted to the EU. The first problem is that a realistic analysis of power relations and the state of democracy in the EU indicates that the "wishes" of business leaders and capitalists, in the Kaleckian sense, have become entrenched in the prevailing EU culture, vested interests and institutional arrangements, make change difficult. Even if some member states may conclude that progressive changes are needed, and even when some rethinking and learning occurs within the Commission, the cumbersome structure of the Union makes it exceedingly difficult to implement new ideas (Patomäki 2014).

The second problem is that the EU is for many purposes comparable to some of the largest states in the world economy. As much as a EU-wide capital tax could do in Europe, from a global perspective it would be no more than a "national" solution – potentially vulnerable to the exit options of capital provided by economic globalization.

There is a better way, however. The enhanced cooperation procedure can be globalized. Any coalition of willing countries can start a system of global taxation by negotiating a treaty, which establishes a system of taxation and a new organization to govern the tax and some of its revenues.[9] The system can be designed in such a way as to encourage outsiders to join. If the idea is to regain democratic control over globalized financial capitalism, the tax system must be democratic. A global tax organization could combine, in a novel way, principles of inter-state democracy (council of ministers), representative democracy (representatives of national parliaments in its assembly) and participatory democracy (civil society representatives). This would make it open to different points of view; capable of reacting rapidly to unexpected changes; and qualified to assume new tasks if needed. Alternatively, a directly elected body is possible as well.

By way of conclusion: the need for global Keynesian economic policies

Is it true that a single global tax would suffice to cure the ills of capitalist market economy? In chapter sixteen, "The Question of Public Debt" (540–70), Piketty discusses various questions of European and world economic policy: the appropriate role of a central bank; whether inflation could be a solution to public debt and the need for redistribution; what kind of common European budget is needed and how it should be organized democratically; and what we should do to control climate change. None of these questions can be reduced to mere income or wealth redistribution. Piketty, too, seems to agree that more is needed than just taxation.

Nonetheless, Piketty's overall argument is geared towards the promise that once wealth is redistributed through the global tax on capital, and via institutions of the social state, the capitalist market economy should work. This excludes questions related to Keynesian demand management. Piketty appears to explain the rate of growth, and especially the current slow growth period in Europe and elsewhere in the OECD, in terms of (i) some sort of normal rate of growth and (ii) a global convergence process in which emerging countries are catching up (72–109). "The history of the past two centuries makes it highly unlikely that per capita output in the advanced countries will grow at the rate above 1.5 percent" (95). Piketty also hints at the possibility that the most recent waves of innovation may have a much lower growth potential than earlier waves (94); and notes that while in the service sector productivity growth has been slow or non-existent, nowadays some 70–80% of the workforce in the developed world works in this sector (90).

These are all plausible hypotheses and possible partial explanations, but as explained in this chapter, they exclude Keynesian concerns about aggregate effective demand, nationally, regionally and globally. The lack of effective demand is the source of many contradictions in the global political economy. For instance, states may be committed to improving their current account balance by enhancing "competitiveness". Yet current account deficits and surpluses cancel out and, moreover, attempts to increase cost competitiveness through internal devaluation tend to prove contradictory due to decreasing effective demand. Moreover, in contrast to positive catch-up processes that almost automatically even out development across the planet, post-Keynesian economists have stressed the equal importance of self-reinforcing tendencies towards uneven and contradictory trajectories of developments (e.g. Kaldor 1972, 1996).

These and other contradictions in the global political economy can be resolved by means of collective actions and by building adequate common institutions (Patomäki 2013, 164–93). For instance, it is possible to build a mechanism through which world trade surpluses and deficits are automatically balanced through tax-and-transfer along the lines of the Keynes-Davidson plan and a global central bank that can issue reserve money (see Davidson 1992–93; Davidson 2004; Stiglitz 2006, 245–68). Such institutions can be characterized as global Keynesian, framing questions of public economic policy and politics on the world economic scale. Global Keynesianism aims to regulate global interdependencies to produce stable and high growth, employment and welfare for everyone everywhere, simultaneously. To put it in Pikettian terms, a well-functioning global Keynesian system could make a big difference in terms of whether $r > g$ or $g > r$.

A well-functioning global Keynesian system would require several new institutions. Reforms may be piecemeal, and proceed through coalitions of the willing, but are not necessarily separate. Processes are connected and interwoven, ideally forming an evolutionary process of mutual facilitation. Hence, it may become increasingly evident that global warming requires global Keynesian responses, such as a democratically organized global greenhouse gas tax and world public investments, rather than a cap-and-trade system premised on the market. Accumulation of relatively small changes in specific areas may lead to ruptures and sudden transformations in others, as issues and processes are often linked.

Using this insight, a series of feasible political economy reforms can also be forged into a strategy of democratic global Keynesian transformation. After a critical point, directional change can become reinforcing, and this may also be deliberately purposed. In a best-case scenario, one world-historical developmental path would be replaced by another.

Notes

1 See Pressman in Morgan (2016, 613–14): Suppose that a person starts out with $100,000 in inherited wealth and $100,000 in yearly labour income. If she receives a 5% return on her wealth, and her wages increase at a rate of 1% per year, then after 100 years her labour income would be $268,000 but her wealth assets would accumulate to $12.5 million and annual income from wealth would be $600,000 – far greater than her labour income.

Piketty's inequality r > g 109

2 Termed "Baumol's disease". Baumol's own solution was to increase the relative funding of sectors where labour productivity does not increase. As many of the services are best produced publicly, this means the expansion of the relative share of the public economy – and, at the same time, more limits to the potential for GDP growth. There is nothing wrong with this development. According to qualitative indicators, it is likely to mean an increase in sustainable welfare, though such connections must be empirically demonstrated. See Baumol and Bowen (1966) and Baumol (2012).
3 Meadows, Randers, and Meadows (2005) update the Club of Rome report. Stern (2006) expects global warming costs to reach several percent of global GDP per year. Over the past few years, studies on the limits to growth indicate that the trends anticipated by the Club of Rome have been becoming actual and that the collapse of industrial production at some point in the 2000s is still a likely scenario (for a good summary of relevant studies, see Wikipedia's http://en.wikipedia.org/wiki/The_Limits_to_Growth # 2002 _30_years).
4 I summarized many of the best-known economic paradoxes and contradictions in Patomäki (2013, ch 2).
5 See Kaldor (1972, 1237–55); for recent analysis of the technology gap in trade and uneven growth, see Cimoli and Porcile (2011).
6 In mainstream economics, it is widely acknowledged that poorer households have higher "marginal propensities to consume". One obvious implication is that any fiscal stimulus targeted toward individuals in the bottom half of the wealth distribution would be more effective than a blanket stimulus. (Carroll, Slacalek, and Tokuoka 2014; Carroll et al. 2016)
7 The dominance of finance changes business behaviour. Businesses will become increasingly concerned about making quick profits and at the same time increasing their market value. The aim is to reduce short-term costs and one effect is to reduce long-term fixed investment and original long-term R&D activities. Empirical evidence supports theories about the decline in real investment. (Palley 2008; Treeck 2009a, 2009b)
8 Capitalist market economies tend to be ones where financial capital and financial resources increasingly dominate politico-economic dynamics. In the past, it may have been learned that speculative financial markets are unstable. Therefore, many forms of speculation are forbidden. As industrial economies grow, and as business resources grow and the power of capitalist interests are strengthened in society, trust that good times will continue forever gets stronger. Deregulation is demanded in the hope of faster profits. When the opportunity and profit opportunities that are opened seem attractive, a positive feedback loop is generated: further deregulation will be required. Countries can also try to use quick returns from financial markets as a competitive advantage. See Minsky (2008).
9 For a more detailed analysis of such a possibility, see Patomäki (2001, chs 5–7) and Patomäki and Denys (2004).

References

APSA Task Force on Inequality and American Democracy. 2004. *American Democracy in an Age of Rising Inequality*. The American Political Science Association. www.apsanet.org/portals/54/Files/Task%20Force%20Reports/taskforcereport.pdf.
Baumol, William J. 2012. *Cost Disease: Why Computers Get Cheaper and Health Care Doesn't*. New Haven: Yale University Press.

Baumol, William J., and William G. Bowen. 1966. *Performing Arts: The Economic Dilemma: A Study of Problems Common to Theater, Opera, Music and Dance*. New York: The Twentieth Century Foundation.

Carroll, Christopher D., Jiri Slacalek, and Kiichi Tokuoka. 2014. "The Distribution of Wealth and the Marginal Propensity to Consume." Working Paper Series No. 1655, Household Finance and Consumption Network, European Central Bank, March. www.ecb.europa.eu/pub/pdf/scpwps/ecbwp1655.pdf.

Carroll, Christopher D., Jiri Slacalek, Kiichi Tokuoka, and Matthew N. White. 2016. *The Distribution of Wealth and the Marginal Propensity to Consume*. Department of Economics, John Hopkins University, December. www.econ2.jhu.edu/people/ccarroll/papers/cstwMPC.pdf.

Cimoli, Mario, and Gabriel Porcile. 2011. "Global Growth and International Cooperation: A Structuralist Perspective." *Cambridge Journal of Economics* 35 (2): 383–400.

Davidson, Paul. 1992–93. "Reforming the World's Money." *Journal of Post Keynesian Economics* 15 (2): 153–79.

Davidson, Paul. 2004. "The Future of the International Financial System." *Journal of Post Keynesian Economics* 26 (4): 591–605.

Galbraith, James, and Béatrice Halbach. 2016. "A Comparison of Top Income Shares and Global Inequality Datasets." The University of Texas Inequality Project Working Paper No. 73, August 22, 2016. http://utip.lbj.utexas.edu/papers/UTIP%2073.pdf.

Gill, Stephen. 1992. "The Emerging World Order and European Change." In *The Socialist Register*, edited by Ralph Miliband and Leo Panitch. London: Merlin Press.

Gill, Stephen. 2008. *Power and Resistance in the New World Order*. 2nd ed. Houndmills, Basingstoke: Palgrave Macmillan.

Gilovich, Thomas. 1993. *How We Know What Isn't So: Fallibility of Human Reason in Everyday Life*. New York: The Free Press.

Harvey, David. 1990. *The Condition of Postmodernity: An Enquiry into the Origins of Cultural Change*. Oxford: Blackwell.

Harvey, David. 2005. *A Brief History of Neoliberalism*. Oxford: Oxford University Press.

Kaldor, Nicholas. 1966. *Causes of the Slow Growth in the United Kingdom*. Cambridge: Cambridge University Press.

Kaldor, Nicholas. 1972. "The Irrelevance of Equilibrium Economics." *Economic Journal* 82 (328): 1237–55.

Kaldor, Nicholas. 1996. *Causes of Growth and Stagnation in the World Economy*. Cambridge: Cambridge University Press.

Kalecki, Michał. 1943. "Political Aspects of Full Employment." *Political Quarterly* 14 (4): 322–31.

Keynes, John M. 1937. "The General Theory of Employment." *The Quarterly Journal of Economics* 51 (2): 209–223.

King, J. E. 2017. "The Literature on Piketty." *Review of Political Economy* 29 (1): 1–17.

Knibbe, Merijn. 2014. "The Growth of Capital: Piketty, Harrod-Domar, Solow and the Long Run Development of the Rate of Investment." In *Piketty's Capital in the Twenty-First Century*, edited by Edward Fullbrook and Jamie Morgan, 156–88. Milton Keynes: College Publications.
Korpinen, Pekka. 1981. *Kriisit ja pitkät syklit* [Crises and Long Cycles]. Helsinki: TTT.
Krugman, Paul. 1979. "Increasing Returns, Monopolistic Competition, and International Trade." *Journal of International Economics* 9 (4): 469–79.
Krugman, Paul. 1980. "Scale Economies, Product Differentiation, and the Pattern of Trade." *The American Economic Review* 70 (5): 950–9.
Krugman, Paul. 1981. "Intraindustry Specialisation and the Gains from Trade." *The Journal of Political Economy* 89 (5): 959–73.
Meadows, Donella H., Jorgen Randers, and Dennis L. Meadows. 2005. *Limits to Growth: The 30-Year Update*. London: Earthscan.
Mihalyi, Peter, and Iván Szelényi. 2016. "Wealth and Capital: A Critique of Piketty's Conceptualisation of Return on Capital." *Cambridge Journal of Economics*, bew054. doi: https://doi.org/10.1093/cje/bew054.
Minsky, Hyman. 2008. *Stabilizing an Unstable Economy*. New York: McGraw Hill.
Morgan, Jamie. 2016. "Understanding Piketty's Capital in the Twenty-First Century." *Review of Political Economy* 28 (4): 612–18.
Oxfam. 2017. *An Economy for the 99%: It's Time to Build a Human Economy That Benefits Everyone, Not Just the Privileged Few*. Briefing Paper, January. www.oxfam.org/sites/www.oxfam.org/files/file_attachments/bp-economy-for-99-percent-160117-en.pdf.
Palley, Thomas I. 2008. "Financialization: What It Is and Why It Matters." Working Paper No. 525, The Levy Economics Institute. www.levyinstitute.org/pubs/wp_525.pdf.
Patomäki, Heikki. 2001. *Democratising Globalisation: The Leverage of the Tobin Tax*. London and New York: Zed Books.
Patomäki, Heikki. 2008. *The Political Economy of Global Security: War, Future Crises and Changes in Global Governance*. London: Routledge.
Patomäki, Heikki. 2013. *The Great Eurozone Disaster: From Crisis to Global New Deal*. London: Zed Books.
Patomäki, Heikki. 2014. "Can the EU Be Democratised? A Political Economy Analysis." In *The European Union and Supranational Political Economy*, edited by Riccardo Fiorentini and Guido Montani, 116–32. London: Routledge.
Patomäki, Heikki. 2017. "Review of *Capitalism: Competition, Conflict, Crisis*, by Anwar Shaikh." *Journal of Critical Realism*, first published online June 1 2017. doi: http://dx.doi.org/10.1080/14767430.2017.1332807.
Patomäki, Heikki, and L. A. Denys. 2004. "Draft Treaty of Global Currency Transactions Tax." In *About Globalisation: Views on the Trajectory of Mondialisation*, edited by Bart de Schutter and Johan Pas, 185–203. Brussels: Brussels University Press.
Pierson, Paul. 2004. *Politics in Time: History, Institutions and Social Analysis*. Princeton: Princeton University Press.

Piketty, Thomas. 2014. *Capital in the Twenty-First Century*. Translated by Arthur Goldhammer. Cambridge: The Belknap Press (of Harvard University Press).
Rawls, John. 1973. *A Theory of Justice*. Oxford: Oxford University Press.
Shaikh, Anwar. 2016. *Capitalism: Competition, Conflict, Crisis*. Oxford: Oxford University Press.
Stern, Nicholas. 2006. *The Economics of Climate Change: The Stern Review*. Cambridge: Cambridge University Press.
Stiglitz, Joseph E. 2006. *Making Globalization Work: The Next Steps to Global Justice*. London: Allen Lane.
Syll, Lars Pålsson. 2014. "Piketty and the Limits of Marginal Productivity Theory." In *Piketty's Capital in the Twenty-First Century*, edited by Edward Fullbrook and Jamie Morgan, 63–74. Milton Keynes: College Publications.
Treeck, van Till. 2009a. "The Macroeconomics of 'Financialisation', and the Deeper Origins of the World Economic Crisis." IMK Working Paper No. 9. www.boeckler.de/pdf/p_imk_wp_9_2009.pdf.
Treeck, van Till. 2009b. "The Political Economy Debate on 'Financialization': A Macroeconomic Perspective." *Review of International Political Economy* 16 (5): 907–44.
Varoufakis, Yanis. 2014. "Egalitarianism's Latest Foe: A Critical Review of Thomas Piketty's Capital in the Twenty-First Century." In *Piketty's Capital in the Twenty-First Century*, edited by Edward Fullbrook and Jamie Morgan, 35–62. Milton Keynes: College Publications.
Wolin, Sheldon S. 2010. *Democracy Incorporated: Managed Democracy and the Specter of Inverted Totalitarianism*. Princeton: Princeton University Press.
Wright, Noah. 2015. "Data Visualization in Capital in the 21st Century." *World Economic Review* (5): 54–72. http://wer.worldeconomicsassociation.org/files/WEA-WER-5-Wright.pdf.

6 Conclusion

Holoreflexivity and the shape of things to come

> Civilization is in a race between education and catastrophe. [...] We cannot tell yet how much of the winning of catastrophe still remain to be gathered in. New falsities may arise and hold men in some unrighteous and fated scheme of order for a time, before they collapse amidst misery and slaughter [...]. Yet, clumsily or smoothly, the world, it seems, progresses and will progress.
>
> H. G. Wells, *Outline of History*, "The World after the Great War" ([1920] 1931, 1169)

Aside from Brexit and potentially Grexit; the conflict in Ukraine involving Russia, the EU, NATO and the US; and Trump's presidency, the world is beset by many similar disintegrative developments. Within the EU, conservative national–populist forces have turned Poland and Hungary increasingly authoritarian. National Front France secured 34% of the vote in the second round of the French presidential elections May 2017, more than any previous election. The military *coup d'état* attempt and its repressive aftermath in Erdogan's Turkey have all but ended EU membership talks. Turkey now verges on dictatorship.

Shinzo Abe, Japanese Prime Minister since 2012, expresses nationalism by, for example, advocating more proactive defence policies and encouraging revisionist stories of Japan's twentieth-century history. Though the extent of his nationalism is controversial, Abe's policies have been part of the increasingly tense East Asian security complex. National–populist developments can be observed elsewhere, for example in Indonesia, becoming particularly marked during the 2014 presidential election and under the subsequent Widodo administration; and in the Philippines, since Duterte was elected President May 2016. Right-wing nationalism and populism are not just a Western phenomenon.

From the viewpoint of my analysis in this book, the cases of China and India are more difficult to explain. The two most populous countries have gone through a period of rapid economic growth. Why should they experience a shift toward nationalism and, in the case of India, also toward exclusive Hindu-populism? The Bharatiya Janata Party (BJP) has existed for decades, preceding the era of growth, and is somewhat comparable to Putin's United Russia. But it is also analogous to the convergence of social forces in Britain that led to Brexit. The BJP-led coalition has supported neoliberal globalization and related policies. One aspect of Indian economic growth is that Western multinational corporations have moved many of their activities to India, contributing to economic growth. India is the second most inegalitarian country in the world and disparities there are growing. As the caste system and other reifications of class differences fade away, rising resentment is directed against different, lower or threatening others, not unlike in Europe, the US and China.[1]

China's President Xi Jinping's nationalistically assertive foreign policy combines with advocacy of free trade and globalization, in a context of securing the state's strong regulatory and fiscal capabilities. In China the rate of investment and saving is very high, which means that consumption has risen modestly in relation to growth (the share of final household consumption declined continuously from 70% in 1962 to 36% in 2007 and has grown only very marginally since then, whereas in the world as a whole this share remains at around 58%).[2] Moreover, the Gini coefficient has risen from roughly 0.3 in the 1980s to 0.49 in the mid-2010s, with the richest 1% of households already owning a third of the country's wealth.[3]

While economic growth and its positive effects for the growing middle and upper classes have provided legitimacy to the ruling party, and while GDP per capita has continued to rise rapidly, since 1997 the Chinese GPI (Genuine Progress Indicator) has improved only slightly (Kubiszewski et al. 2013, 61–2). This indicates that even in China $r > g$ may hold in some sense. Economic improvements may also have spurred expectations about democratization. A plausible hypothesis is that the Chinese leadership has resorted to the "rally-around-the-flag" effect, habitually articulated in terms of overcoming "the century of humiliation" whilst expressing the rising power of a "harmonious nation" and growing economy, to gain legitimacy.

From a global political economy perspective, all these developments are interconnected. A part of the story is that capital is exercising exit options, which often means that activities are diffusing from (what used to be) the core to (what used to be) the periphery. Changing power relations resonate with the global relocation of industrial and other economic activities. As a result, the core resorts to cost reduction and deflationary economic policies to retain industrial and other activities as much as possible, while the periphery relies on expansive strategies of export orientation. Soon interlocked vicious and virtuous circles start to transform what is core and what is periphery. "The pace and pattern of global growth is conditioned by 'under-consumption' in some regions of the world and 'over-borrowing' in other regions" (Cripps, Izurieta, and Singh 2011, 232). This imbalance would seem to favour countries like China, but reality is more complicated. Chinese under-consumption diminishes global aggregate demand and thus weakens economic growth potential (in China the Kaldor-Verdoorn effect may dominate but not forever). The global imbalance predisposes the world to financial and other crises, which not only affect China but may also start there. Moreover, the first part of the Polanyian double movement involves increasing inequalities and commodification in China and other rising economies, which tend to have political repercussions through mechanisms I set out Chapters 2–5.

The main point is that market globalism is not sustainable. After a period of liberalization toward what Polanyi called the stark utopia of free markets, global interconnectedness tends to generate disintegrative tendencies. Spatio-temporal processes are multiple. Sometimes they are mutually reinforcing, but they can be elongated, disjoint, intersecting, overlapping and contradictory. Throughout this book I have suggested that there is a tendential rational direction to world history – grounded in institutionally enabled and facilitated existential security and trust – toward global Keynesianism, global social justice and global democracy.[4] A move in this direction requires new levels of personal and institutional reflexivity and organizational complexity, especially on a planetary scale.

Reflexivity means the capacity of actors to reflect – in consciousness and discourse – on their own conditions and place such that both can change. Holoreflexivity means that one can see oneself as an active part of a dynamic whole. Holoreflexivity involves a holistic analysis of mechanisms, structures and processes which is not only global but also planetary: "It is global in that it encompasses all social groupings, communities, cultures and civilisations, and planetary in that it comprises the totality of relationships between the human species and the rest of the biosphere" (Camilleri and Falk 2009, 537). My overall argument is that holoreflexivity is the next *rational* step in the mutually reinforcing processes of complexification and increasing reflexivity, and that there is a real tendency toward that direction.[5]

In the rest of this concluding chapter, I first discuss briefly three elements of rationality that constitute movement toward holoreflexivity and global Keynesianism, justice and democracy. I bring the book to a close by outlining the shape of things to come by discussing scenarios about possible and likely futures for the EU and for the whole world system. These are big themes and space is limited, but my analysis of disintegrative tendencies in the global political economy would be incomplete without considering the possibilities for enlightenment in the twenty-first century.

On the rational tendential direction of world history

Three elements of rationality constitute the tendential directionality of world history. The first is truth, involving criticism of falsehoods and attitudes that sustain falsehoods. The second concerns overcoming contradictions through collective action and common institutions. And the third involves normative universalizability and our capacity to resolve social conflicts.

Criticizing falsehoods

Truth and social scientific explanations have normative and political implications. It is of course not possible to know the world except under certain geo-historical, transient descriptions, but rational judgements about those descriptions are nonetheless possible.[6] Consider the beliefs of a typical voter for "Leave" in the UK 2016 referendum or for Trump in the US 2016 Presidential elections. There is a divergence between the real causes of the conditions they criticize and the stories they tell or take for granted about those conditions. Falsehood is never categorical, but always a matter of degree. All sufficiently consistent and comprehensive points of view have a non-zero status of validity; and even more limited perspectives can contain a grain of truth. Although the main elements of the geo-historical complex causing austerity, slackening growth, rising inequalities and erosion of democracy have little to do with migration, it is nonetheless true that with specific institutional and market arrangements and economic circumstances, migration can put downward pressure on local wages or employment (Gietel-Bastein [2016] talks about a toxic mix of immigration and austerity). At the same time, we know that high levels of migration and rapidly rising wages can be fully compatible, as demonstrated by the history of the United States or Australia, or European cases such as Sweden and Germany from the 1960s to 1980s. A point of view, or a claim, with a non-zero but limited status of validity can nevertheless be false in an essential sense (non-accurate, based on generalization of some aspect of a context-specific case, lacking explanatory power, misleading, illusionary, mystifying etc).

The same holds true for many metaphors, background assumptions and cognitive schemes accepted by a typical voter for "Leave" or for Trump. A metaphor may be apt (and in that sense true) because it structures one's real experience. It is a metaphor to conceptualize time as a resource and time as money; in capitalist market society, this metaphor is constitutive of practices and thus structures our experiences (e.g. wage-earners are paid according to the amount of time they work). And yet even apt metaphors can be misleading and in important regards false.[7] If we only work for money and our work has no intrinsic value, the result is alienation. Similarly, the family-metaphor can structure many experiences of the nation. We may feel it is good to be back "home" when arriving at a busy airport of a city where we do not live, with millions of people we do not know, but we can become aware of how relative that experience can be (or how easily it can be extended to other places). In the same way, the assumption that there is a fixed amount of work to be done within a national economy may look locally plausible under conditions of austerity, zero or negative growth, and high levels of unemployment, but it fails as a general explanation of available employment opportunities.[8]

We can also criticize ignorance, indifference and illusions, which contribute to asymmetrical relations of power and heteronomous determinations. Hegel's ([1910] 2003, ch IV.B) famous distinctions between different subservient attitudes to power continue to illuminate this problematic (here I rely as much on Bhaskar 1994, 1–3, 81–94). The first attitude Hegel considers is that of the Stoic, who purports to be indifferent to the reality of the world. In explicit thinking, or in imagination, one is free and equal, but not in actual social practices and relations. Stoic unconcern can also result from prosaic cynicism: "I do not care; and what difference would my voting make anyway?" What the "Stoic" tries hard to ignore, the more advanced Sceptic (or contemporary postmodern relativist, who can declare there is nothing outside the unstable and constantly changing systems of signs) attempts to deny. But both the Stoic and the Sceptic end up in a theory/practice contradiction. What they try to ignore or deny, they approve in practice. Laws ground private property that they must respect; institutional and market arrangements and economic circumstances dominate their lives; and they do acknowledge that a privileged few can easily translate money into power and *vice versa* in ways that also affect them.

The Unhappy Consciousness emerges when one sees all this, but imagines another world, perhaps an after-world, where the reality of prevailing circumstances and relations of dependency are overcome. She may be religious,[9] but in the contemporary world the compensation for disappointing reality often comes in a fantasy world of sport, soap, nostalgia etc. In the twenty-first century, commercial media such as Fox News and tabloids such as the *Sun* combine scandals, sport, soap and nostalgia with nationalism and neoliberalism.[10] In an increasingly unequal society, a few billionaires are likely to emerge (including figures such as Trump), keen to pour generous funding into the Tea Party, the "Leave" campaign or Trump's election campaign. Money buys visibility and influence.

In this context, the Unhappy Consciousness may come to adopt the master's ideology, although the aim was to find solace in games, fiction and fantasy. When agitated by the consequences of economic crises or otherwise traumatically changing circumstances, this Unhappy Consciousness has the potential for being transformed into angry anti-establishment politics. The paradox is that this kind of anti-establishment politics is framed in terms of the masters' preponderant ideology. The emotional stance may have real grounds, but the response is misguided because of false ideological beliefs (based at a deeper level on economic theory and political philosophy). Although falsehoods may be relative, they are real.

Overcoming contradictions

More and better knowledge can make an important difference. Notably, knowledge can be about practical contradictions that tend to defeat the overt purpose of actions and policies. Contradictions in this sense can arise from incorrect beliefs about how things work (e.g. if one mistakes a poisonous substance for medicine) or from the lack of generalizability (e.g. if everyone simultaneously attempts to avoid losing money by withdrawing all their savings from a vulnerable bank). The latter is a case of fallacy of composition, leading through self-fulfilling effects to a bank run. Finally, contradictions can occur at the level of social systems, if there are organizing principles that work against each other (e.g. a Keynesian welfare state can be contradictory in an open and liberal world economy, where corporations can move their tax base elsewhere). Real-world contradictions are not categorical because whether the contradicting forces cancel each other out – or whether one force in the end annuls the other – depends on contingent circumstances (e.g. how much poison one takes; how many individuals are withdrawing their savings simultaneously; what factors other than taxation determine investment decisions).

Many contradictions can be overcome by collective action and by building adequate common institutions. As discussed on several occasions in Chapters 2–5, neoliberal states' economic policies are contradictory in various ways. The attempts by states to be more "competitive" or "secure" than other states, or to have balanced budgets or ensure long-term fiscal sustainability, tend to result in self-defeating outcomes. Consider the case of world trade. The compositional fallacy occurs when it is assumed that what is possible for a single given actor at a given time is possible for all simultaneously. Overall, trade deficits and surpluses always cancel out, so it is impossible that most states would be simultaneously running surpluses. Over time, countries with trade surpluses tend to also accumulate savings surpluses, whereas countries with trade deficits tend to accumulate debt, resulting in global financial imbalances. Therefore, simultaneous attempts by all or most states to improve their trade balance can be contradictory. The likely overall result is a general reduction in effective aggregate demand in the world economy.

Keynes's (1942, 1943) plans for a Clearing Union involved an impartial system for the management of currencies, and a kind of world central bank responsible for a common world unit of currency, the bancor. Obligations would be made systemic, with financial positions defined against the rest of the world, not individual countries. At first Keynes proposed that surpluses beyond a given amount would be fully confiscated for a global fund. His later, more modest formulations included mechanisms for transferring resources from surplus to deficit countries. A key idea was to enable a "New Deal" within every country, including full employment.

The 1944 Bretton Woods agreement did not include a world central bank or bancor or system of taxing the surplus. Instead, the IMF started to demand deflationary conditions on its loans. A few years after the end of the Bretton Woods era (1944–1973), the Third World debt crisis erupted. Both the IMF and the World Bank started to apply structural adjustment policies to crisis countries. The burden of adjustment was shifted onto deficit countries, frequently resulting in deep recession, high social costs and further accumulation of debt.

In this context, Keynes's original proposal was renewed and developed further by the Brandt Commission (1980) and, most notably, by Davidson (1992–93, 2002, 2004). Davidson updated Keynes's plan to meet twenty-first-century circumstances with a more moderate version that requires neither a gold-based currency system nor a world central bank. Davidson's version is to some degree more nationally oriented than Keynes's original plan, and a supranational central bank is not necessary and, "at this stage of economic development and global economic integration, [. . .] not politically feasible" (2002, 209). Davidson's plan involves a spectrum of different capital controls (as did Keynes's original). A country can only be living beyond its means if it is at full employment, but its deficit may still be due to poverty, in which case richer countries are obliged to help. The system is thus redistributive. If a member country accumulates excessive credit balances by running current account surpluses, it has three options to spend its credits: "(1) on the products of any other member of the clearing union, (2) on new direct foreign investment projects, and/or (3) to provide unilateral transfers (foreign aid) to deficit members" (Davidson 2004, 600).

Stiglitz (2006, 245–68; based on earlier edition of Greenwald and Stiglitz 2010) outlines a prominent version of the Clearance Union plan. Stiglitz (with Greenwald) proposes a Global Monetary Authority and "global greenbacks", an idea that comes closer to Keynes's original proposal than Davidson's version. Stiglitz holds the current dollar-system partly responsible for prevailing global financial instability. A jump to a new system based on an alternative national currency such as the euro or yuan renminbi would not solve the problem. A new global reserve system could finance global public goods; and could demonstrate a commitment by the world community to global social justice (Stiglitz 2006, 266). Hence the Stiglitz–Greenwald version introduces new ethical and political principles. Variations among the proposed schemes stem from differences not only in economic theory but also in ethical and political principles.

Ethical and political learning

Contradictions can be overcome by collective action and by building adequate common institutions, but the emergent question – exactly what institutions would be more adequate? – involves many ethical and political considerations. Ethical and political learning concerns reasoning about social rules and principles. The more adequate the cognitive scheme of reasoning is for human cooperation and for resolving conflicts, the better it is. Normatively, a key consideration is the degree of generalizability – indicating acceptability and stability of judgements in differentiated and complex multi-actor contexts – and the related capacity for abstract role-taking. The self learns to assume the role and perspective of others. Higher-stage reasoning is more differentiated (implying a more nuanced understanding of social realities) and more integrated (implying symmetry and consistency) than prior stages.[11]

The conflict in Ukraine has been moulded and conditioned through and triggered by political economy processes, but at one level it is also a clash between different "just causes" for war. Theories that give meaning to the basic metaphor of justice typically select one or a few models of justice, interpret and apply them in a particular way and exclude other models and their possible interpretations and applications. These biases and exclusions tend to legitimize asymmetric power relations. They may also generate conflicts. Conceptions of justice can clash, and clashes may escalate into violence. Furthermore, there is a strong tendency to fall back to lower levels of moral reasoning under the stress of open conflict, due to the operation of various psychological conflict avoidance mechanisms. Violence and war can have far-reaching consequences on moral learning (see Habermas 1979, 91–3). The problem is acute when actors narrativize experiences and social episodes in terms of good, justice and order on the one hand, and evil, injustice and chaos on the other, thus drawing unconsciously on mythic symbolic structures of heroism or Manichaeism that give meaning to human life and death (see Aho 1990). Collective evolutionary progress is realized in institutional mechanisms for resolving conflicts and deciding upon rules and principles.

Differentiated and generalizable self–other dynamics, and adequate moral reasoning, depend on the recognition of plurality of competing conceptions of justice. Common institutions must be built accordingly. Rational dialogue on different models of justice is possible, but dialogical rationality means relativism. Epistemological relativism (which is consistent with ontological realism and the possibility of rational judgements and learning) means that we cannot trust anybody to know a priori, or with too much certainty, what models of justice to follow. Epistemological relativism is one of the main arguments for democracy. Without free speech, adequate public spaces for critical dialogue and equal access for all to collective will formation, any community may be led astray, including the world community. There is also the spectre of a vicious circle of the accumulation of power in the hands of powerful actors, groups or coalitions, just because they are powerful and can thus unilaterally shape prevailing moral conceptions, rules, principles and practices. Hence, an argument for global justice is decisively also an argument in favour of global democratization (see Patomäki 2006; Held and Patomäki 2006).

Following (i) criticism of falsehoods and (ii) proposals to overcome contradictions through collective action and common institutions, global democracy is the third signpost that establishes rational directionality to emancipatory processes in the current geo-historical conjuncture. Global democracy is about normative universalizability and the capacity to resolve social conflicts. Philosophical and political theoretical discussions can take the complex process of human learning further. For many theorists in the late twentieth century, the most advanced scheme of ethico-political reasoning seem to correspond to Rawls's (1971) principles of democratic justice, but many critics – Frankfurt School theorists, post-structuralists and critical realists – have pushed the debate forward by arguing that the Rawlsian conception is monological, and propose dialogical and differentiated alternatives.[12]

Habermas (1990, 197) formulates the basic principles of discourse ethics, including "only those norms can claim to be valid that meet (or could meet) with the approval of all affected in their capacity as participants in a practical discourse". Derrida (1988, 1992) emphasizes the constructed and open character of identities and shows how easy it is to fix one's identity, in ways with potentially (perhaps metaphorically) violent effects. He also points to difficulties of creating ethico-political spaces free from asymmetrical or biased power relations. Derrida's interest lies in the conditions for a democracy to come, in which justice means thorough mutual respect for the other, all subjects reflexively understanding that their subjectivities are effects of language and world history.

Bhaskar (1993, 1994) in turn wants to draw attention to the multilayered non-discursive conditions of fulfilling the universal norms of free ethico-political discourse. Any possible approximation of the norms of free discourse is always contingent upon many politico-economic, educational, ecological and other real conditions, and these must be considered in institutional design.

On the shape of things to come: nodal points and possible futures

In contrast to Hegel's belief that what is rational is real and what is real is rational, the real and the rational are only contingently related. Enlightenment in the twenty-first century requires geo-historically situated critique and transformative praxis. What emerges from the discussions of Chapters 2–5 is that the global financial crisis has been a world history nodal point. It has been a saddle point, inducing stasis and regression. Ten years ago I assumed (Patomäki 2008) that the election of George W. Bush as US President and the rise of explicitly neo-imperialist discourse would be a major turning point. Retrospectively, it has no doubt shaped Russian politics (resonating with its internal political dynamics), provoking a gradual turn in the orientation of the Putin regime, but otherwise its immediate impact has been more limited than I anticipated. Instead, the global financial crisis and its second phase, the Euro crisis, have turned out to be a watershed in the development of disintegrative tendencies both in Europe and in the whole global political economy. It is time to update scenarios about the shape of things to come, first in the EU, then globally.

Three scenarios about the future of the EU

Trust in the EU has declined, in part due to a prolonged economic downturn and crisis (with deep roots in the global financialization process), but in part because of what is perceived to be the technocratic, undemocratic or unchangeable nature of the EU. Exclusive processes of identity politics, securitization and enemy-construction also stem from existential insecurities. However, the future of the EU depends to a significant degree on future economic developments. Precise predictions are not possible in open systems. Despite the EMU-driven tendency towards low investment and high unemployment, and despite expectations of a new major financial crisis by 2020, a lot depends on the precise budget positions and timing and nature of the next downturn or crisis. Even a relatively short-lived semi-recovery of the European economy would give time for the EU to evolve in novel directions, and semi-recovery is exactly what seems to be happening in Europe in 2017. Also, the Brexit-mess and Emmanuel Macron's election in May 2017 have soothed the situation.

The current EU strategy is to tighten the Union under the rubric of enhancing its external competitiveness. In practice, this amounts to austerity; further market-based "reforms"; budget and labour market discipline (coupled with labour market "flexicurity"); internal devaluation and perhaps also currency devaluation; flimsy banking union; and development of elements of modest common fiscal capacity.

These policies feed into the first phase of the mechanism depicted in Figure 3.3. The explicit idea, however, is to increase demand for European goods and services in world markets – at the expense of other countries. As noted, world imports and exports cancel out; their overall sum is always zero. In Varoufakis's (2016, 240) estimation, "to escape its crisis in this manner the Eurozone must reach a current account surplus in relation to the rest of the world of no less than 9 per cent of total European income". This is unlikely to succeed, but if it succeeded, it would "destroy the hopes of America, China, Latin America, India, Africa and South East Asia for stability and growth". The estimate of 9% is sketchy, a rough estimate of the needed scale, which depends on the rapidly changing economic context, but the argument is sound.

There is more than one possible future for the EU, however. One possibility is an increasingly disciplined and militarized Union. Common external enemies can spur unity. Perhaps the exit of Britain will facilitate consolidation of the remaining EU via escalating conflict with Russia, the constant "state of emergency" related to the refugee crisis and imagined or real terrorist attacks (often by migrant sufferers of class inequalities), increasingly strained relations with Turkey, economic competition with China and India, and the global consequences of Trump?

The two-phase mechanism presented in Figure 3.3 can also be exploited to further a common European cause, which is something that is already happening in 2017. The identification of threats to "our European" existence can create unity and acceptance, or at least acquiescence, to strengthening the disciplinary rule and military nature of the EU. The Trump administration demands more military spending by EU member states, but it also erodes trust in the transatlantic alliance. This increases the likelihood of the scenario of a military/security-based EU. From a cosmopolitan perspective, one of the ambiguities of the Union has always been the possibility that it generates a nationalism of its own and evolves into a military great power. What is more, expanding security and military spending significantly could boost the European economy. By pooling part of this spending through EU institutions, and perhaps by introducing EU taxes, the Union could manage to create some common fiscal capacity.

This scenario may not be the most likely, but it is becoming more probable. The Euro crisis distracted from developing a common European security and defence policy, but that phase of the Euro crisis is over. While the US and NATO, together with EU member states, remain the main players vis-à-vis Russia, and while the process of building an increasingly disciplined and militarized Union would take time, with several propitious circumstances coinciding and coalescing, attempts to construct such a union might succeed. The EU would then be on par with the USA, Russia, and China, a military superpower in the global insecurity community (as anticipated by Galtung [1973]. The global insecurity community can be further destabilized by new downturns and crises in the world economy. A new global power-balancing system between continent-based regional alliances would not necessarily be very different from the European past. This is not a good scenario for the world.

The third possible future would accord with the tendential rational direction of world history. The left cosmopolitan project to transform the Union could succeed at some point in the 2020s. There are various plans to use the resources of the European Central Bank and the instruments of the European Investment Bank to create a public investment programme on a European scale (e.g. Varoufakis, Holland, and Galbraith 2013); and to relieve national budget constraints, for instance by a new application of the so-called Golden Rule, exempting public net investment from the relevant deficit targets (e.g. Truger 2016). These plans do not necessitate changes in the basic treaties of the EU, so they could be implemented rapidly.[13] Moreover, the proposal for a Common Consolidated Corporate Tax Base (CCCTB) could be developed further and taken as a contribution to the EU budget. The procedure of enhanced cooperation could be used with some of the revenues channelled to a common fund or euro-area budget. These steps could explicitly ground Treaty revision, creating full fiscal capacities for the EU.[14]

Apart from a diluted CCCTB (CCTB), none of these proposals is on the EU agenda in 2017. The first phase of the plan to "complete EMU" was due to be realized by summer 2017 and the last phase by 2025. If a will emerges to change the course of EU economic policy, it will take at least a year to start implementing even a modest plan. What is more, the proposed – and even more so, the realistically achievable – scale of required expansion in public spending appears rather limited. Doubling the level of European Investment Bank lending or gradually adding about 1% of GDP deficit funding to public investments would boost the European economy to a degree, and these public investments could contribute to European reindustrialization, but all this may turn out too little too late. At best, these plans could buy time. The realization of the DiEM25 scheme to democratize the Union would take time too.

I know only one way to deliberately speed up the process: the use of citizens' initiatives and referenda on the euro and related fiscal discipline.[15] In any case, the purported DiEM25 first step is to achieve full transparency in decision-making. Written in autumn 2015, the manifesto demands that this should be realized within a year. More realistically, it is conceivable that transparency could become one theme of European Parliament elections in 2019. Its successful implementation is yet another matter – as is whether EU citizens want it. The second demand is to convene "an Assembly of citizens' representatives' within two years. Nothing like this is on the agenda in 2017. The Euro crisis and Brexit may have prepared the ground for revisiting and revising the Treaty of the EU in certain regards, but even in the best of circumstances, to initiate this kind of process would take at least 2–4 years. Currently, there is no political will to establish a directly elected constitutional assembly. If anything, the EU has become more intergovernmental and German-dominated during the Euro crisis, and this may be difficult to reverse except in terms of securitization.

The current policies, principles and institutions of the EU generate counterproductive politico-economic effects and suffer from problems of legitimacy. These effects and problems, which are not confined to Europe, give rise to tendencies towards disintegration. From the rational directionality point of view, the problem is the timing of the required learning and reforms, especially in view of the likelihood of a new global financial crisis. Modest policy proposals and tentative steps within the existing EU Treaty framework may be too little too late. The question is whether there is enough time for deeper transformations in Europe and globally before a new regressive saddle point is reached. It would be better to avoid that point entirely.

Scenarios for the world

Here I can discuss only briefly the two main sets of scenarios for the whole global political economy (cf. Patomäki 2008, 2010). Scenarios are (A) about possible paths that involve disintegrative tendencies and escalation of the emergent conflicts gradually assembling conditions for an ever bigger crisis – or a full-scale global catastrophe. The contrastive scenarios (B) are based on the notion that rational, peaceful and democratic transformations of global governance are possible without a global catastrophe. In subscenario B_1, long-term learning processes, combined with some sort of generic understanding of global threats, will suffice to generate a movement to transform and rebuild the systems of global governance. This movement will eventually also convince some governments to change and create new international and global law. In the more likely scenario, B_2, the same thing will happen only after a series of relatively limited economic crises and wars.

The global financial crisis of 2008–2009 was a saddle point, inducing stasis and regression. At first the crisis prompted some neo-Keynesian measures, but without any significant deviation from the substantive path of neoliberalization in most dimensions of policy (Patomäki 2009). No new worldwide transformative movement emerged, and global civil society remains more marginal for high politics than it was in the aftermath of the Asian crisis (1998–2002). The responses to the 2008–2009 crisis and its repercussions have remained national and contradictory. The crisis was contained, and an arduous recovery of the world economy started in 2010, but was then further and significantly complicated by the euro crisis. Since then, the main responses have become even more liable to contradictions and further disintegration due to the reasons discussed in Chapters 2–5.

After a partial economic recovery, governments, central banks, media corporations and other authorized bodies have been returning to their official policy lines and optimism, grounded in standard neoclassical theory; the bulk of regulators and law-makers have continued to pursue relative state-competitiveness and security at the expense of long-term stability and development, because they do not see any alternative either. As the "recovery followed by business-as-usual" scenario has proven right, the underlying super-bubble that has already lasted for more than three decades continues to grow and will likely gradually create the conditions for an even bigger crash in the late 2010s or, at the very latest, in early 2020s. As argued, the Trump administration's demand for financial deregulation is likely to precipitate this process and make the next financial bust deeper.

There are "weak signals", however, that indicate that the next crisis will not be just another saddle point, inducing further stasis and regression and hastening the process toward a global catastrophe, however likely that may seem now. One is that most young people in Europe or North America do not support right-wing nostalgia, nationalism and populism. Young people have potential for further ethico-political learning. This is the generation that has never seen anything other than neoliberalism. The search for alternatives, perhaps in the context of a series of limited near-future crises, can generate not only new networks and movements but also a search for new forms of political agency. While a transnational public sphere has existed since the mid-nineteenth century, a new kind of reflexively political global civil society emerged in the late twentieth century. Attempts to create wider civil society coalitions and to forge forms of global political agency have been largely unsuccessful.

In Patomäki (2011) I argue that transformative political agency presupposes a shared programme, based on common elements of a wider and deeper world-view, and a willingness to engage in processes of collective will-formation in terms of democratic procedures. From this perspective, I outline a possible organization and some substantial directions for a global political party. The point is also to respond to the criticism of existing parties and cultivate the critical-pluralist ethos of global civil society, but in terms of democratic party-formation. Independently of this idea, the brief and weak spell of official neo-Keynesian learning that emerged in 2009 indicates that even within established sites of power, progressive learning can occur quite spontaneously. The next round of politicization may already be different.

Moreover, the institutions of governance associated with global scale are not necessarily more difficult to transform than those associated with more limited scales. The stasis of the EU is also due to its institutional design, which makes it highly resistant to any transformation. It is very difficult to change the EU, as its current institutional arrangements are "locked in" by neo-constitutional means, whereas it can be relatively easy to create new global institutions through a grouping of states. Any new world organization can be established, at first, by a grouping of like-minded countries, like the International Criminal Court was in the 1990s. Thus, it may be possible to achieve relatively rapid progress with a group of like-minded states, even though the aim must be a truly global organization.

The final conclusions

Once again, civilization is a race between education and catastrophe. The Industrial Revolution led to the unifying influence of economic globalization, and yet "catastrophe won – at least to the extent of achieving the Great War" (Wells [1920] 1931, 1169). A century later, we may ask in the Wellsian spirit: how much of the winning of catastrophe remains to be gathered in? Many of the trends that we are observing are not particularly promising in this regard, at least not in the short or medium run. Disintegrative tendencies in the global political economy will dominate developments in the late 2010s and early 2020s, increasing the likelihood of a catastrophe, but these developments are complex and contingent, and there are countertendencies.

Most importantly, the tendential rational directionality of world history is grounded on universal human learning processes. For instance, as life expectancy has increased from 52 in 1960 to 72 in 2016, life is, in general, valued more highly than ever (think of how the death penalty is fading away), which is indicative of ethical and political learning. Furthermore, even amidst the apparent dominance of disintegrative tendencies, the processes of globalization continue to alter our way of being in the world and propel us towards a cosmopolitan outlook (Beck 2016).

It seems that what we are witnessing in the late 2010s is a dialectic between three logics of identity and community. First, from the standpoint of neoliberal market globalism, differences and communities are hard to see. The economistic logic of this form of globalism precludes any explicit ethical and political considerations. Everyone must be identical and submit

128 Conclusion

to market globalism and its characteristic modes of thin subjectivity (e.g. calculative egoism, consumerism, resilience) and its characteristic socio-economic effects (involving inequalities, etc.).

Second, as argued in this book, various political economy processes can accentuate differences into intensely and perhaps violently negative self-other relations. The concerns and anxieties of everyday life have the potential to be mobilized for antagonistic politics against both globalism and associated forms of otherness, such as immigrants. This mobilization occurs in terms of frames, categories, metaphors and myths that have been sedimented into the deep structures of national and religious imaginaries (cf. Patomäki and Steger 2010), from where they are again being drawn, also out of anxiety and for various strategic purposes.

The third logic is reflexive and concerns recognition and equality. Demands for recognition and equality will continue to diversify claims and open new possibilities. These demands can politicize market globalism in terms of problematizing the privileges and inequalities characteristic of market globalization. It is realized that there are other ways to organize democracy and relations of production and exchange, promoting trust and existential security.

In this chapter, I have argued that holoreflexivity is the next rational step in the processes of complexification and increasing reflexivity, and that there is a real tendency towards that direction. Proposals for a global tax on capital and global Clearance Union exemplify what this movement can mean in practice. The processes of complexification and increasing reflexivity will evoke new imaginaries, identities and forms of political agency, which accord with contemporary scientific myths and truth-claims and with underlying and emerging ethico-political sentiments. The key task of future global reformers will be to ensure that evolving global rules and institutions will be made, and will remain, democratically transformable.

Notes

1 For example, "Inequality in India: what's the real story?", 4 Oct 2016 World Economic Forum column by Nisha Agrawal, the CEO of Oxfam India, available at www.weforum.org/agenda/2016/10/inequality-in-india-oxfam-explainer/. I am thankful to Professor Samaddar, Calcutta Research Group, Kolkata, for illuminating discussion on the political situation in India. See also Samaddar (2016).
2 World Bank data, household final consumption expenditure, etc. (% of GDP), available at http://data.worldbank.org/indicator/NE.CON.PETC.ZS?locations=CN.
3 Figures based on a January 2016 Beijing University report, widely cited in the world press (e.g. http://thediplomat.com/2016/01/report-chinas-1-percent-owns-13-of-wealth/). Different datasets give different figures.
4 See Bhaskar for the tendential rational directionality of geo-history concept (1993, 158–64, *et passim*). He argues "absence will impose the geo-historical

Conclusion 129

directionality that will usher in a truly humane human global society, mediated by explanatory critical and emancipatory axiological social science". I have developed the argument that currently the rational direction is toward democratic global Keynesianism (Patomäki 2013, ch 8, 2014a). More broadly what matters is not any particular end state, but the objective process of human emancipation, in which there are numerous different and historically evolving possibilities and participants, each with their authentic stories about the prevailing situation and desired direction. See discussion below concerning notions of truth and democracy.

5 Complexification involves many qualitatively different elements, their functional differentiation and interconnectedness and emerging properties at various levels of organization. Camilleri and Falk (2009, 535–58). New properties at higher level of organization do not imply *per se* that the highest level will become the dominant spatial scale within a system of multi-spatial meta-governance, to use Jessop's (2012) expression.

6 According to Bhaskar (1979, 80), one is justified in characterizing a belief or theory as "ideological" if both (i) some relevant aspects or elements of that belief or theory are false; that is, one possesses a superior explanation for the phenomena; and (ii) one possesses an explanation of the falsity of the beliefs in question and why they are held. From this follows a negative evaluation of those practices and structures that produce or sustain the false beliefs or theories. For a sympathetic but critical reconstruction of this scheme of explanatory emancipation, see Patomäki (2002, ch 6).

7 Vico (1668–1744) first argues in *The New Science* (1725) that metaphors and narratives may be true. Underlying this claim is Vico's famous *verum ipsum factum* principle, which states that truths can be invented and constructed (this idea does not contradict scientific realism or the definition of truth as correspondence). Lakoff and Johnson (1999, 72–3) discuss the aptness and truth of metaphors – metaphors can also have entailments that can be literally true or false – the Time Is a Resource and Time Is Money metaphors: "It is true that in this society we have to budget our time. It can be true that someone can waste an hour of our time" (164).

8 Mainstream liberal economics applies critique of the lump of labour fallacy to claim that it is not possible to raise the minimum wage without hurting employment (see Patomäki forthcoming), or that shortening the working day does not translate into more jobs. But the basic insight of economics that while immigration increases labour supply, it also increases demand for labour, is valid. Moreover, when migrants work, they also produce value and contribute to economic expansion. This does not mean that very high levels of immigration could not cause economic, social and ecological disturbances even in the best of economic circumstances; nor does it mean that the effects of migration would not depend on location, social positioning, policies and institutional arrangements. About the latter, see for instance the briefing of The Migration Observatory of the University of Oxford, available at www.migrationobservatory.ox.ac.uk/resources/briefings/the-labour-market-effects-of-immigration/.

9 See note 7 of Chapter 1.

10 In discussing whether it is possible to democratize the EU I have suggested: "Commercial media power is largely based on advertising. This suggests that taxing advertising at a high rate, the game can be smoothed out and funds diverted towards supporting public media. The tax rate on mere image advertising could

be set at 100 per cent and the tax on other forms of advertising at 50 per cent. The tax could be agreed within the Union or, more preferably, globally. National authorities would collect the tax. A part of the revenues collected in Europe should go to financing a public pan-European media company, which could operate via the satellites and the Internet, but may also be able to develop print outlets as well. Its explicit task would be to further democracy and cultivate principles and virtues of good public journalism." (Patomäki 2014b, 126)

11 Here I am most indebted to Kohlberg's (1971, 1973) "From Is to Ought: How to Commit the Naturalistic Fallacy and Get Away with It in the Study of Moral Development" and "The Claim to Moral Adequacy of a Highest Stage of Moral Judgment", republished in Kohlberg (1981). Kohlberg died in 1987, but subsequent research has confirmed, method-independently, the existence of a common scheme of development of moral reasoning and judgement, and related social perspective-taking, across a variety of cultural and politico-economic contexts (Boom, Wouters, and Keller 2007; Dawson 2002; Gibbs et al. 2007; see also Robinson 2007).

12 The more dialogical and differentiated alternatives do not imply endorsement of greater inequalities than Rawls's (1971). Rawls's democratic difference principle prescribes, among other things, that differences in socio-economic position and expectations should be allowed only if they improve the situation of the least favoured. "Inequality in expectation is permissible only if lowering it would make the worst-off social class even more worse off" (78). Rawls considers his position to be more egalitarian than that of utilitarianism (implying also that the argument according to which incentives and innovations require inequalities is fairly weak). All readings of Rawls's principle are geo-historically specific; usually the incentive-argument presupposes that selfishness and greed are the accepted social norms, which of course is a contingent, context-dependent social occurrence

13 Galbraith, Meyer, and Patomäki (2016) start from the premise that immediately implementable reform proposals must be consistent with the Treaty of the European Union. We list various plans to use the resources of the European Central Bank and the instruments of the European Investment Bank to create a public investment programme on a European scale; and to relieve national budget constraints for instance by implementing a Golden Rule approach, exempting public investment from relevant deficit targets. We further complement these with several proposals to democratize Union practice. However, a more essential transformation of the EU requires changing the EU Treaty.

14 This proposal is related to the idea of a global capital tax. Corporate tax has fallen dramatically (tens of percent) in most countries. In addition, large multinational companies engage in aggressive tax planning, which further reduces tax revenues by at least a hundred billion euros a year in the EU. The EU has not been of any assistance in overcoming the tax war between member states. If anything, the tax "competition" has been more severe in Europe than elsewhere or globally. For four scenarios about realizing the CCCTB, see http://patomaki.fi/en/2017/03/toward-a-common-european-corporate-tax-and-full-eu-fiscal-capacity-four-scenarios/.

15 Civil society organizations and interested political parties could use the mechanism of citizens' initiative to call simultaneously for referenda in the EU as a whole and within member states. A lot hinges on design of the referenda. A referendum should include multiple choices – the third option being the cosmopolitan Left's alternative – and the voting system could be

designed to include multiple preferences (there are different methods of doing this). For further details, please see http://patomaki.fi/en/2016/01/beyond-plan-b-and-c-on-the-use-of-citizensinitiative-and-referenda/.

References

Aho, James. 1990. "Heroism, the Construction of Evil, and Violence." In *European Values in International Relations*, edited by Vilho Harle, 15–28. London: Pinter.

Beck, Ulrich. 2016. *The Metamorphosis of the World*. Cambridge: Polity Press.

Bhaskar, Roy. 1979. *The Possibility of Naturalism: A Philosophical Critique of Contemporary Human Sciences*. Brighton: Harvester Press.

Bhaskar, Roy. 1993. *Dialectic: The Pulse of Freedom*. London: Verso.

Bhaskar, Roy. 1994. *Plato Etc: Problems of Philosophy and Their Resolution*. London: Verso.

Boom, Jan, Hans Wouters, and Monika Keller. 2007. "A Cross-Cultural Validation of Stage Development: A Rasch Re-Analysis of Longitudinal Socio-Moral Reasoning Data." *Cognitive Development* 22: 213–29.

Brandt, Willy. 1980. *North-South: A Programme for Survival: The Report of the Independent Commission on International Development Issues under the Chairmanship of Willy Brandt*. London: Pan Books.

Camilleri, Joseph A., and Jim Falk. 2009. *Worlds in Transition: Evolving Governance across a Stressed Planet*. Cheltenham: Edward Elgar.

Cripps, Francis, Alex Izurieta, and Ajit Singh. 2011. "Global Imbalances, Under-Consumption and over-Borrowing: The State of the World Economy and Future Policies." *Development and Change* 42 (1): 228–61.

Davidson, Paul. 1992–93. "Reforming the World's Money." *Journal of Post Keynesian Economics* 15 (2): 153–79.

Davidson, Paul. 2002. *Financial Markets, Money and the Real World*. Cheltenham: Edward Elgar.

Davidson, Paul. 2004. "The Future of the International Financial System." *Journal of Post Keynesian Economics* 26 (4): 591–605.

Dawson, Theo Linda. 2002. "New Tools, New Insights: Kohlberg's Moral Judgement Stages Revisited." *International Journal of Behavioural Development* 26 (2): 154–66.

Derrida, Jacques. 1988. *Limited Inc*. Translated by Alan Bass and Samuel Weber. Evanston, IL: Northwestern University Press.

Derrida, Jacques. 1992. *The Other Heading: Reflections on Today's Europe*. Translated by Pascale-Anne Brault and Michael B. Naas. Bloomington: Indiana University Press.

Drezner, Daniel W. 2015. "Targeted Sanctions in a World of Global Finance." *International Interactions: Empirical and Theoretical Research in International Relations* 41 (4): 755–64.

Eagleton-Pierce, Matthew. 2016. *Neoliberalism: The Key Concepts*. London & New York: Routledge.

Fukuyama, Francis. 1989. "The End of History." *The National Interest* (16 Summer 1989): 3–18.

Galbraith, James K., Henning Meyer, and Heikki Patomäki. 2016. *Governance of the EU: Problems and Reform Proposals*. Progressive Economy Initiative e-Publications (S&D Group of the European Parliament). www.progressiveeconomy.eu/content/governance-eu-problems-and-reform-proposals.

Galtung, Johan. 1973. *The European Community: A Superpower in the Making*. London: George Allen & Unwin.

Gibbs, John C., Karen S. Basinger, Rebecca L. Grime, and John R. Snarey. 2007. "Moral Judgment Development across Cultures: Revisiting Kohlberg's Universality Claims." *Developmental Review* 27: 443–500.

Gietel-Bastein, Stuart. 2016. "Why Brexit? The Toxic Mix of Immigration and Austerity." *Population and Development Review* 42 (4): 673–80.

Greenwald, Bruce, and Joseph E. Stiglitz. 2010. "Towards a New Global Reserve System." *Journal of Globalization and Development* 1 (2): 1–24.

Habermas, Jürgen. 1979. *Communication and the Evolution of Society*. Translated by Thomas McCarthy. Boston: Beacon Press.

Habermas, Jürgen. 1990. *Moral Consciousness and Communicative Action*. Translated by Christian Lenhardt and Shierry Weber Nicholsen. Cambridge: MIT Press.

Harmes, Adam. 2012. "The Rise of Neoliberal Nationalism." *Review of International Political Economy* 19 (1): 59–86.

Hegel, G. W. F. 2003. *The Phenomenology of Mind*. Translated by J. B. Baillie. This translation was first published in 1910 and the original in German in 1807. Mineola, NY: Dover Publications (Dover Philosophical Classics).

Held, David, and Heikki Patomäki. 2006. "Problems of Global Democracy: A Dialogue." *Theory, Culture & Society* 23 (5): 115–33.

Jessop, Bob. 2012. "Obstacles to a World State in the Shadow of the World Market." *Cooperation and Conflict* 47 (2): 200–19.

Kagarlitsky, Boris. 2017. Brexit and the Future of the Left, *Globalizations* 14 (1): 110–117.

Keynes, John M. (1942) 1969. "Proposals for an International Currency (or Clearing) Union [February 11 1942]." In *The International Monetary Fund 1945–1965: Twenty Years of International Monetary Cooperation, Volume 3: Documents*, edited by J. Horsefield, 9–18. Washington, DC: International Monetary Fund.

Keynes, John M. (1943) 1969. "Proposals for an International Currency (or Clearing) Union [April 1943]." In *The International Monetary Fund 1945–1965: Twenty Years of International Monetary Cooperation, Volume 3: Documents*, edited by J. Horsefield, 19–36. Washington, DC: International Monetary Fund.

Kohlberg, Lawrence. 1971. "From Is to Ought: How to Commit the Naturalistic Fallacy and Get Away with It in the Study of Moral Development." In *Cognitive Development and Epistemology*, edited by Theodore Mischel, 151–235. New York: Academic Press.

Kohlberg, Lawrence. 1973. "The Claim to Moral Adequacy of a Highest Stage of Moral Judgment." *Journal of Philosophy* 70 (18): 630–46.

Kohlberg, Lawrence. 1981. *The Philosophy of Moral Development: Moral Stages and the Idea of Justice: Essays on Moral Development Volume 1*. San Francisco: Harper & Row.

Conclusion 133

Kubiszewski, Ida, Robert Costanza, Carol Franco, Philip Lawn, John Talberth, Tim Jackson, and Camille Aylmer. 2013. "Beyond GDP: Measuring and Achieving Global Genuine Progress." *Ecological Economics* 93: 57–68.

Lakoff, George, and Mark Johnson. 1999. *Philosophy in the Flesh: The Embodied Mind and Its Challenge to Western Thought*. New York: Basic Books.

Mikko, Salmela, and Christian von Scheve. 2016. "Emotional Roots of Right-Wing Political Populism." *Social Science Information*, accepted for publication, available at https://www.academia.edu/31722166/Emotional_roots_of_right-wing_political_populism

Minsky, Hyman. 2008. *Stabilizing an Unstable Economy*. New York: McGraw Hill.

Patomäki, Heikki. 2002. *After International Relations: Critical Realism and the (Re)construction of World Politics*. London: Routledge.

Patomäki, Heikki. 2006. "Global Justice: A Democratic Perspective." *Globalizations* 3 (2): 99–120.

Patomäki, Heikki. 2008. *The Political Economy of Global Security: War, Future Crises and Changes in Global Governance*. London: Routledge.

Patomäki, Heikki. 2009. "Neoliberalism and the Global Financial Crisis." *New Political Science* 31 (4): 431–42.

Patomäki, Heikki. 2010. "Exploring Possible, Likely and Desirable Global Futures: Beyond the Closed vs. Open Systems Dichotomy." In *Scientific Realism and International Relations*, edited by Jonathan Joseph and Colin Wight, 147–66. London: Palgrave.

Patomäki, Heikki. 2011. "Towards Global Political Parties." *Ethics & Global Politics* 4 (2): 81–102. www.ethicsandglobalpolitics.net/index.php/egp/article/view/7334.

Patomäki, Heikki. 2013. *The Great Eurozone Disaster: From Crisis to Global New Deal*. London: Zed Books.

Patomäki, Heikki. 2014a. "On the Dialectics of Global Governance in the 21st Century: A Polanyian Double Movement?" *Globalizations* 11 (5): 751–68.

Patomäki, Heikki. 2014b. "Can the EU Be Democratised? A Political Economy Analysis." In *The European Union and Supranational Political Economy*, edited by Riccardo Fiorentini and Guido Montani, 116–32. London: Routledge.

Patomäki, Heikki. 2015. "Absenting the Absence of Future Dangers and Structural Transformations in Securitization Theory." *International Relations* 29 (1): 128–136.

Patomäki, Heikki. forthcoming. "The Ideal of Competitive Markets: On the Social Psychology and Politics of Neoclassical Theory." *Under Review of Cambridge Journal of Economics*.

Patomäki, Heikki, and Christer Pursiainen. 1999. "Western Models and the Russian Idea: Beyond Inside/Outside in the Discourses on Civil Society." *Millennium: Journal of International Studies* 28 (1): 53–77.

Patomäki, Heikki, and Manfred Steger. 2010. "Social Imaginaries and Big History: Towards a New Planetary Consciousness?" *Futures* 42 (10): 1056–63.

Rawls, John. 1971. *A Theory of Justice*. The original ed. Cambridge, MA: Belknap Press (Harvard University Press).

Reynolds, David. 2017. "Britain, the Two World Wars and the Problem of Narrative." *The Historical Journal* 60 (1): 197–231.

Robinson, Paul H. 2007. "The Origins of Shared Institutions of Justice." *Vanderbilt Law Review* 60 (6): 1633–88.

Samaddar, Ranabir. 2016. *A Post-Colonial Enquiry into Europe's Debt and Migration Crisis*. Singapore: Springer.

Stiglitz, Joseph E. 2006. *Making Globalization Work: The Next Steps to Global Justice*. London: Allen Lane.

Truger, Achim. 2016. "The Golden Rule of Public Investment: A Necessary and Sufficient Reform of the EU Fiscal Framework." IMK Working Paper No. 168. Dusseldorf. https://ideas.repec.org/p/imk/wpaper/168-2016.html.

Varoufakis, Yannis. 2016. *And the Weak Suffer What They Must? Europe, Austerity and the Threat to Global Stability*. London: The Bodley Head.

Varoufakis, Yannis, Stuart Holland, and James K. Galbraith. 2013. *A Modest Proposal for Resolving the Eurozone Crisis – Version 4.0*. www.yanisvaroufakis.eu/modest-proposal/.

Watkins, Susan. 2016. "Casting off?" *New Left Review* (100): 5–31.

Wells, H. G. (1920) 1931. *Outline of History: Being a Plain History of Life and Mankind*. The new and revised ed. New York: Garden City Publishing.

Index

Abe, S. 113
Albright, M. 83
altercasting 59
Amadae, S. 30
American Political Science Association (APSA) 70, 104
anti-establishment politics 20, 130
arms races 6
Asia 11, 51, 60, 126
Asian financial crisis 1997–98 51, 126
austerity 22, 26, 28, 53, 86, 101, 117, 123
Australia 86, 116
automatization 34, 75–6, 85

banking sector 21–2
Bannon, S. 83
Barkawi, T. 48
beggar-thy-neighbour policies 9, 84–5
Bharatiya Janata Party (BJP) 114
Bhaskar, R. 117, 121, 128, 129
boom-and-bust process 9, 47, 52, 87
Braithwaite, J. 82
Brandt Commission 119
Bretton Woods 4, 41, 16–17
Brexit 1, 7, 16–40, 114, 125
BRICS 82
Bull, H. 3–4, 89
bureaucratic regulations 77
Bush, G. W. 122

Cameron, D. 16–17, 20, 22, 35
capitalism 34, 97, 99; financial 96, 107
capitalist: domination 6, 90; economic system 6, 21, 42, 45–7, 55, 73, 80, 89, 104; market economy 47, 107; market society 89, 94, 101–2, 116; peace 42–5, 47, 57 (*see also* liberalism, liberal-capitalist peace); power of capitalist interests 109; relations of production and exchange 101, 128; world economy 9, 11, 21, 73
China 2, 11, 27, 60, 71, 99–101, 113–15, 123–4
City of London 20–1, 33
Clearance Union plan 119
clearing union 119
climate change 84, 107–8
cognitive schemes 23–7, 116, 120
collective learning 10–11, 73, 82–3, 120–1, 126
Colour Revolution 51–2, 58, 63
commodification 36, 46, 97, 115
Common Consolidated Corporate Tax Base (CCCTB) 124, 130
competitiveness 5, 9, 19, 86, 90, 101, 107–8, 123, 126
complexification 115, 128–9
comprehensive accountability 62
concentration of wealth and power 50, 55, 94, 96, 103–5
Conservatives 16, 18, 20, 22, 28, 33–4
Corbyn, J. 30, 35
cosmopolitan: democracy 35, 62; left 7, 20–1, 124, 131; orientation 20; outlook 127
Cox, R. 82, 90
Crimea 56–8, 60
critical responsiveness 61

Davidson, P. 108, 119
Davies, James C. 54–5, 63
de-democratization 50, 105
deflation 6, 31, 96, 100–2, 114, 119
deindustrialization 18, 22, 24, 27, 29, 49, 96, 99
demand: aggregate efficient 10, 47, 64, 86, 95, 100–1, 107–8, 115, 118
democracy: cosmopolitan 35, 62; de-democratization 50, 103, 105; global 11, 20, 61, 121; and peace 42, 45, 48–9, 57, 62; and reforms of global governance 20, 49, 62, 115, 121, 125, 128, 129; social 30
democratic: deficit 24; peace 42, 45, 48–9
Democratic Party 30–1, 127
Derrida, J. 121
Deutsch, K. 43, 61
DiEM25 124–5
disintegration 3, 31, 87, 125
Dodd-Frank Act 87
double standards 8, 60–2, 71, 77, 84–5
Doyle, M. W. 48
Drahos, P. 82
Duterte, R. 113

East-Asian security complex 113
economies of scale 46, 100
economic: activities 97, 114; anxiety 29; changes 23, 78; circumstances 17, 23, 27, 116–17, 129; conditions 5–6, 22, 56, 59, 96, 116–17, 122; context 43, 123; developments 21–5, 31–3, 61, 77, 102, 122; differences 20, 61; difficulties 32, 59; disaster 42, 96–105; divergence 96, 100; domination 33, 36, 80, 90; downturn 12, 22, 54–6, 99, 122, 124; elite 18; equalities/inequalities 4, 11, 18, 21–3, 36, 46, 50, 55, 87, 94–6, 100–3, 128; freedom 50; globalization 106; growth 5, 9, 12, 52, 94, 99, 101, 114–15; hardship 55; interests 45–6, 76; liberalism 6, 19, 21, 102; man 29; nationalism 87; paradoxes 109; policy 24, 96–7, 99–100, 107–8, 124; power 78; practices 49, 63; problems 5–6, 26, 47; relations 6; sanctions 43, 58–60; shock 42, 49, 103; situation 50; success 46; system 8, 70, 80; tendencies 29; theory 26, 78, 118, 120; treaties 3, 104; troubles 24, 55, 59, 77; uncertainties 55; waves 97–9, 107
economic crises 48, 94, 105, 117, 125; Asian financial crisis 1997–98 51, 126; global financial crisis 2008–2009 4, 20–1, 22, 32, 43, 52–3, 58, 70, 72, 75, 103, 125; Great Depression 48
emotion: emotional distancing 7, 24, 25, 55–6; powerful 25, 33
enemy-construction 12, 56, 59, 64, 105, 122
Engels, F. 7
Erdogan, R. T. 7, 113
Euro crisis 7
European Central Bank (ECB) 19, 32, 35, 124, 130
European Commission (EC) 20, 49, 106
European Economic Community (EEC) 41, 78
European Monetary Union (EMU) 31–2, 35, 62, 122, 124
European Neighbourhood Policy (ENP) 41–5, 49
European Union (EU): Association Agreement with Ukraine 55–6; budget 44, 107, 124; competitiveness 9, 86, 123, 126; democracy-promotion 41, 52; economic policy 24, 32, 42–3, 63; EU-nationalism 123–4; expansion 42, 51–2, 57; fiscal capacity 123; Memorandum on Greece's debt 7; neighbourhood policy 41–4, 49, 52, 57–8, 61; as a neoliberal project 20, 41; scepticism about 19; self-righteous universalism 8, 60–2; treaty 17–24, 31, 41, 125
Eurozone 31–2, 123
Evola, J. 83
exercise of power 10, 73
existential: guilt 25–7, 30; insecurity 2, 5, 11, 23–4, 55–6; security 115, 128; shame 25–7, 30; uncertainty 24, 33, 54, 70, 77

fallacy: of composition 4–6, 47, 118; lump of labour 26, 129
false universalism 61–2
financial: boom (*see* boom-and-bust process); bubble 87, 126; bust (*see* boom-and-bust process); capitalism 96, 107; crash;87; crisis 2008–2009 32, 52, 72, 103; deregulation 9, 19, 86–7, 109, 126; elites 23; imbalances 61, 118; instability 101, 119, 126; investors 3; multiplication 87; sanctions 59; stability 9, 87, 126; taxes and regulation 20; transaction tax (FTT); transparency 106
financialization 6–7, 52, 87, 96–7
Finland 34, 60
fiscal policies 32, 83, 119, 123–4
Fox News 117
France 17–18, 113
free market utopia 19, 27, 51, 61, 105, 115
French presidential elections 2017 113
Friedman, M. 19, 42
functional cooperation 41

G20 106
Galtung, J. 3, 41, 59, 124
game theory, Prisoner's Dilemma 80–1
General Agreement on Tariffs and Trade (GATT) 19, 101
general election, British 16, 21, 28, 34
Genuine Progress Indicator (GPI) 35
geo-politicization 43
Georgia 51–2
Germany 17, 29, 46, 116, 125
Giddens, A. 12
Gilpin, R. 78–9, 89
Gini coefficient 35, 50, 114
global: central bank 108; change 84; common good 72; constitutionalism 104; cooperation 87; debt problem 95; democracy 11, 20, 61, 121; disaster 64, 96, 105; disorder 81; economic system 8, 70, 80; economy 101 (*see also* capitalist, economic system; world economy); financial stability 87; free market 19, 33; governance 125–8; greenhouse tax 108; institutions 60, 82, 88, 127;

leadership 77–8; money 20, 119; political economy 41, 62, 82, 94–6, 108, 114–15, 122, 127; political party 126–7; public good 79; recession 85; rifts 106; rule of law 44, 62; security 79; social justice 20, 115, 120; south 48; tax 97, 105–7, 128; tensions 51; war 1, 102–4, 127
global catastrophe: ecological 2; military 2, 62, 88, 96, 113, 125, 126–7
Globalization 3, 22–4, 27–8, 33–4, 70, 75–6, 105–6, 114, 127–8
global Keynesianism: institutions 118–20; policies 20, 96–7, 105–7, 123–7
Global Monetary Authority 119
golden age of capitalism 99
golden rule of diplomacy 61
good governance 42, 44, 49, 62
Great Depression 48, 78
great powerness: EU as a military great power 123–4; great power conflicts 4, 105; great power pluralism 51
Great Transformation 29–30
Greece 7, 21, 32
Gross Domestic Product (GDP): criticism 22, 97
Grunberg, I. 2, 72, 89

Haas, P. 81–2
Habermas, J. 6, 55, 89, 120–2
hegemonic: common sense 73; leader 71, 77–8, 80–1; non-hegemonic cooperation 81; post- 80, 82; power 72; stability theory 77–80; state 71; US 77–82; war 79
hegemony, after 80–1; *see also* US hegemony
heterodox economists 46, 99
high-income countries 96–9
historical analogy 6, 12
Holland 17
holoreflexivity 10–11, 113, 115, 128
Hungary 9, 113

identity-politics 5–6, 17–18, 24–5, 32, 55–6, 90, 104, 121
Ikenberry, J. 82
immigration 16–18, 23, 26–7, 116, 129

impersonal markets 77
India 2, 11, 86, 99, 101, 113–14, 123, 128
Indonesia 113
industrialization 2, 24, 34
inequality: and accumulation of privileges 24; fundamental 94; and global war 102–4, 127; growing 4, 35, 94–102; income 35, 74; reduces consumer demand 101; and returns on capital as a function of initial wealth 50, 94; rising 29; in the US 73–5; wealth 50, 70–5, 94–104
inflation 101–2; asset price 95
insecurity: community 124; existential 2, 5, 11, 23–4, 55–6, 124
integration: European 4, 16–18, 20, 31; meaning 94; social 55
international law 3, 57, 60, 84, 104, 125
International Monetary Fund (IMF) 19, 53–4, 64, 119
international political economy 1, 45
inverted totalitarianism 104–5
investments 5, 78, 83, 86, 95, 100–1, 108–9, 118, 124, 130
Iran 59
Ireland 21, 32

Japan 86, 95, 113
Jessop, B. 129

Kaldor-Verdoorn effect 100, 115
Kalecki, M. 46, 104, 106
Keohane, R. 72, 80–1
Keynes, J. M. 46, 80, 100, 119
Keynes-Davidson plan 108
Keynesian: demand management 107; economic policy 97, 99, 101; global- 20, 61, 108, 115, 127; Keynesian-Kaleckian economic-theoretical point of view 9, 11; military 6, 9; multiplier 100–1; neo- 125, 127; post- 46, 108; public expenditure 100; welfare state 118
Kindleberger, C. P. 47, 78–80
Korpinen, P. 101
Kosovo 51, 57
Krasner, S. D. 78–9
Krugman, P. 46, 100

labour market 26, 29, 70, 123
Laffey, M. 48
Lafointane, O. 20
Latin America 2, 123
Lavrov, S. 51
left: cosmopolitan 7, 21, 131; exit 7; left/right divide 20; New 77; -orientation 20; responses 30
Lexit 7, 20
liberalism: liberal-capitalist peace 42, 45–8, 57; liberal capitalist world economy 73; liberal-democratic peace 42, 48–9, 57; neo- 19–21, 23, 27, 33–4, 52–3, 58, 61–2, 101–2, 127–8
Libertarianism 19, 33
limits to growth 96, 109
Lisbon Treaty 17
List, F. 46
London: City of 20–1, 33

Maastricht Treaty 19, 21, 24, 31–2, 41
manufacturing: consent 33; and economies of scale 100; employees and real output 21; jobs in 75; share of 2, 75–7, 85; value added 75; value of production 76
market right-orientation 20
Marx, K. 7, 46
Mayhew, A. 76–7
media 1–3, 25, 28, 30, 32, 33, 36, 56, 73, 89, 117, 126, 130
Mélenchon, J. L. 30
mental illness 70
metaphor 26–7, 97, 116–17, 129
middle class 2, 9, 75, 101, 114
Middle East 1, 4
monetarist economic policies 19, 101
Morgenthau, H. 61
Moser, J. 9, 48, 84
Mundell, R. 21
Murdoch, R. 28

national: fiscal policy 32, 117, 124; goods and services 9, 86; income 21; interests 80, 84; national/cosmopolitan divide 20; national-populist developments 34, 113; orientation 20; powers to limit the movements of people 21, 27; price

levels 97; referenda 17; security apparatus 83; sovereignty 8, 84; states 6; statism 6
National Front France 18, 113
nationalism: and disintegrative politics 7, 18; economic 33, 87, 105, 114; modern 29, 33, 71, 117; and neoliberalism 26, 117; racist 6; in Russia 51, 61
nationalist: movements 30, 34, 113; populism 6, 33, 113–14; -populist 7–20; protectionism 18, 76, 105, 114; right 113; right-wing parties 7, 18, 30; Trump's nationalist-protectionist policies 70–88
NATO 4, 42, 51–2, 63, 124
neoclassical economics 19, 26, 29–30, 35, 42–7, 78, 94–5, 126
neo-constitutionalism 105, 127
neo-Gramscianism 82
neo-imperialism 79, 89, 122
neo-Keynesianism 126–7
neoliberal globalization 7, 33, 102, 114
neoliberalism 6, 19, 30, 41, 52, 61, 70, 78, 95, 101–2, 125–6
neo-revisionism 51–2
New Labour 22, 36
new trade theory 46, 100
Norway 17

OECD 5, 19, 50, 86, 99–100
orthodox economic policy 101–2
Overton Window 16

path-dependence 21, 78, 88
peaceful changes 61–2, 105–8, 125
Pettifor, A. 28–30, 70–1
Philippines 113
Piketty, T. 10, 50, 87, 94–108
Pinker, S. 1, 49
Plan B 20
pluralism 51–2, 60–3
pluralistic security community 61
Poland 62, 113
Polanyi, K. 28–9, 34, 46, 71, 77, 115
Polanyi's double movement 7, 28–9, 70, 88, 90, 100, 115
populism 6, 18, 33, 113–14, 126
populist-nationalist movement and parties 7, 18, 20, 30, 33, 34, 57

Portugal 32
post-Western world 1, 83, 88
power: American 80; asymmetric 19, 76, 117, 120; -balancing 6, 12, 51, 57, 60, 124; changing relations of 95; civilian 58; coercive 48; corporate 102; disparities 70–1, 76, 81, 96, 101, 117, 120; explanatory 52, 129; faces of power 102; hegemon's 72, 78, 79; knowledge/power-positions 89, 104; learning- and power-dynamics 24; narrow 43; of the neoliberal field 101; politics 58; powerful business interests and money 84; power relations in the US 73; Putin's 51; relations between capital and labour 28, 46, 76, 95, 101; state-power argument 78; as transformative capacity 73
precarization 29
Prisoner's Dilemma 80–1
private debt 22, 70, 75
privatization 49, 53, 62, 86
protectionism: external competitiveness 86, 123; international devaluation 86, 108, 123; tariffs 9, 85–6; taxation 86; tax competition 5, 86
public debt 32, 54, 64, 95, 107, 118–19
public opinion 5, 19, 23–4, 26–7, 32–5, 73
Putin, V. 4, 42, 50–1, 57, 59–60, 63, 114, 122

rally around the flag 59–60, 114
rational choice theory 30, 35, 81
Rawls, J. 103, 121, 130
Reagan, R. 19
real-world socio-economic effects 61, 128
referendum 131; British 16, 18, 32, 34, 116; Crimea 68
refugees 25–6
religion 12, 23, 25, 90
renationalisation of politics 21–6, 32
robotization *see* automatization
Russia 4, 8, 42–4, 49–52, 56–63, 71, 88, 94, 122–4

Sakwa, R. 42, 51, 58
Sandel, M. 22

Sanders, B. 73–5
Schneider, G. 47
securitization 2, 12, 43, 52, 55–6, 58, 59, 63, 104–5, 122, 125
security: apparatus 1, 83; collective 4; community 61–2, 124; complex 43, 113; dilemma 4; EU's security and prosperity strategy 45; existential 115, 128; lack of job security 22; margin 6; Marx and 46; Munich security conference 83; policy 42, 58, 83; and protection of property rights 79; security and military spending 123; security order centred on the US 58; threats 58, 123, 125; Trump's foreign economic and security policies 83
self-regulating market 29, 49, 71
Serbia 51
Shaikh, A. 97, 100
social distance 70
social-psychological mechanisms 21, 24, 33, 89
socio-economic divergence 94–6
Soros, G. 84
Soviet Union 2, 48–9, 51–2, 57, 79
Spain 7, 21, 32
Strange, S. 1, 72, 79–80
Sun (tabloid) 28, 117
Sweden 18, 116
Sykes, P. 28
Syrian civil war 4
Syriza 7, 20, 30

Task Force on Inequality and American Democracy 70, 104
tax: on advertising 129–30; aggressive tax planning 3, 130; base 118; on capital 96–7, 105–7, 128, 130; competition 5, 86, 130; corporate 5, 124, 130; cuts 5, 86–7; financial 20, 32–3, 106; global greenhouse gas 108; havens 103; progressive 75, 103; reductions 34, 64, 71; revenues 55, 85, 106; tax-and-transfer 102, 108; Tobin tax 106; Trump's tax reform 71–6, 86–7; on wealth 96–7, 106–7, 128
taxes: on capital 96–7, 105–7, 128, 130; European 106; financial 20, 32–3, 106; global 97; progressive 75, 103; on wealth 96–7, 106–7, 128
Tea Party 77, 117
Technical Assistance to the Commonwealth of Independent States (TACIS) 41
terrorism 1, 34, 58
Thatcher, M. 19–21, 28
Tory Party *see* Conservatives; referendum, British
Trade in Services Agreement (TiSA) 86–7
trade policies 6, 9, 19, 33, 42, 44, 72, 78, 83–6, 100, 104, 118
Transatlantic Trade and Investment Partnership (TTIP) 86
transnational organizations 3, 42, 80–2, 100
Transpacific Trade Partnership agreement (TTP) 86
Triffin Dilemma 80
Trump, D.: America First Trade Policy 85; economic programme 82–8; financial deregulation 86–7; major tax-cuts for corporations and rich 86–7; security policy 84–5
Turkey 83, 113, 123
two-level game 17

UKIP 16–18, 27–8, 30–4
Ukraine: conflict 41–64; current account 53–4; demonstrations 55, 64; Euromaidan 55–6, 63
financial crisis 2008–2009 53, 58; foreign reserves 54
unemployment 4–5, 22–4, 29–31, 54–5, 63–4, 70, 77, 95, 117, 122
United Kingdom 7, 16–36, 75–6, 104, 106, 116
universal health care 26, 75
universalism 51, 61–2
US: double standards 84; federal budget 83, 87; international cooperation 81–5, 88; national interests 84; national sovereignty 84; power 80
US 2016 elections 70–7
US hegemony 77–82, 79–80, 82

Index 141

Varoufakis, Y. 6, 12–13, 20, 95, 123–4
war 1, 4, 6, 8, 10, 41–3, 49, 57–8, 78–9, 103, 105, 120, 127–8
wealth: inequality 35, 74–5; inherited 50, 94–6, 103, 108; tax on 96–7, 106–7, 128
Widodo, J. 113
Wolin, S. 70, 104
working class 18, 29, 55, 70
World Bank (WB) 19, 62, 119; *see also* Bretton Woods
world economy 2, 4–5, 9, 21, 32, 41, 48–9, 61–2, 73, 77–80, 84, 88–102, 118, 126
World Health Organization (WHO) 89
world-historical mechanisms and processes 1–7, 17, 30, 41, 50, 72–3, 82, 88, 95, 100, 102, 107, 115, 121, 128; *see also* world history
world history: and rationality 116–22; tendential directionality 11, 48, 88, 97, 115, 116–28
world order model 57, 60–1, 70–3, 81–2, 88, 90
world public investments 108, 119–20
World Trade Organization (WTO) 19, 82, 85
World War I 6, 46, 103
World War II 17, 41, 48, 70

Xi, Jinping 114

Yanukovych, V. 56
Yeltsin, B. 49–51
Young, O. 81

For Product Safety Concerns and Information please contact our EU representative GPSR@taylorandfrancis.com
Taylor & Francis Verlag GmbH, Kaufingerstraße 24, 80331 München, Germany

www.ingramcontent.com/pod-product-compliance
Lightning Source LLC
Chambersburg PA
CBHW070837020526
44114CB00041B/1948